How to
Receive
and
Release
the
Anointing

BERRY DAMBAZA

WESTBOW
PRESS®
A DIVISION OF THOMAS NELSON
& ZONDERVAN

WestBow Press books may be ordered through booksellers or by contacting:

WestBow Press
A Division of Thomas Nelson & Zondervan
1663 Liberty Drive
Bloomington, IN 47403
www.westbowpress.com
1 (866) 928-1240

ISBN: 978-1-9736-4537-5 (sc)
ISBN: 978-1-9736-4538-2 (e)

Library of Congress Control Number: 2018913485

Print information available on the last page.

WestBow Press rev. date: 12/05/2018

Endorsements

I highly recommend this book by Berry Dambaza. If you have ever desired a greater understanding of the anointing of the Holy Spirit and how you can be used through the anointing to minister to others, this is a must have book. Berry Dambaza who is one of my sons in the gospel makes this book's easy to understand and apply approach a tremendous tool and practical guide on the anointing.

I strongly believe that this book will inspire you into a deeper walk with God. Read this book time and again and most importantly, apply the revelational truths unveiled in this book and experience God's anointing in a fresh way, and enter into a greater dimension of operation in your life and ministry.

Dr. David A Newberry
Tulsa, Oklahoma, USA.

www.davidnewberry.org
http://www.facebook.com/DavidANewberryMinistries

In these days of spiritual confusion and the abuse of the supernatural power and anointing of God by some ministers, Bishop Berry Dambaza's book brings clarity and insight that is important to bringing understanding, maturity and balance to the church in the issue of receiving and releasing the anointing.

Dr. Goodwill Shana

Founder and Senior Pastor of Word of Life International Ministries, President of the Association of Evangelicals in Africa (AEA). Former President of the Evangelical Fellowship of Zimbabwe (EFZ) and past Chairman of the Zimbabwe Christian Heads of Denominations.

www.wolim.org

The anointing is the key to living a supernatural life as a believer. It is the anointing that enables us to do great exploits for God and to minister to people's lives. The ability to have the anointing operate in our lives is what is explored in this book. The book is a great resource for anyone who is eager to learn how to flow in the anointing from a seasoned servant of God who has lived a life of receiving and releasing the anointing. This book will surely be a blessing to you.

C S Tuturu

Prolific Author, Senior Pastor of the Harvest House International Harare City Church and the Apostolic Hub Leader of the Harvest House International Church Mashonaland Region, Harare, Zimbabwe.

www.cstuturu.org

The Holy Spirit is without doubt the Church's greatest asset and secret weapon in our push for the end time harvest. He is the partner for anyone who desires to live a successful life. Without Him, all our efforts at life or ministry are watered down to the point where struggle becomes inevitable.

Critical to effectively functioning in the ministry is an understanding of the anointing and how it works. I am so pleased, in fact thrilled beyond words, that Bishop Dambaza has given us a manual to help us flow in the anointing through this book.

Bishop Dambaza presents a subject that he has experienced during his walk in his ministry journey. The testimonies regarding the anointing are very encouraging and I can attest to the fact that he has understood how to flow in the anointing. He is therefore very well placed to help you maximise the anointing over your life in a way that will benefit you and others in a practical way.

This book is not designed just for the ministers of the gospel but it will benefit any believer who desires to flow in the anointing. Here is my encouragement to you as you read and engage with this wonderful book; Have the heart of a child and be open to receive, not from Bishop Dambaza, but from the Lord who inspired him to write this book.

Have the mind of a student who is ready to grasp the various concepts presented in this book and reap a radical transformation in your heart, mind and life. And finally, have the zeal of a hungry lion in applying the truths you get from this inspiring book.

Refuse to consign the rich wisdom in this book to the archives of your mind but rather mix the Word of God contained therein with faith and see the anointing work wonders in your life and ministry.

May God bless and increase His anointing upon you as you read this book.

Never Muparutsa
Assistant Presiding Bishop/Bishop Designate of the PAOZ and Senior Pastor of PAOZ-
Jubilee Christian Centre, Milton Park, Harare, Zimbabwe.

How To Receive and Release the Anointing is a powerful ministry tool and resource that comes precisely at the right time for our generation. The deceptive spirits of this age have systematically pressured some ministers to pursue strange fires in a quest to find relevance and significance in ministry. This book will stir the minister in the right direction of biblical truth and balance on the subject of the anointing.

This is not just a must read book, but a must have book, that one needs to have and that one refers to time and time again as they grow and develop in ministry. The anointing is the privilege to operate on God's behalf and Bishop Dambaza has given us illuminations and clarity on the dynamics of the anointing. Truly impartation will take place as you read this book and we thank God for His vessel that has answered many questions we have had on the subject of the anointing.

Vukani Dhladhla
Bishop of the Abiding Hope Global Ministries and Chaplain at Corporate Marketplace
Chaplaincy, Author and Life Coach, Harare, Zimbabwe.

If anyone wants to receive the Holy Spirit anointing and to be used in releasing the anointing, this is the book to read as it reveals keys for effective ministry. This book is wonderful,simple and clear in explanation. I believe this book will help believers,ministers of the gospel and other church leaders to move in miracles, signs and wonders!

Yehoshua Mandapalli
Bishop, Jesus Saves Ministries International, Hyderabad, India.

This is a profound and highly enlightening book on the anointing of God. Many are ignorant on how to receive and function in the anointing of God. Having known Bishop Dambaza for 18 years, I can safely say the truths unravelled in this work are a reflection of both what is passionately believed and practiced by him.

This work is a convicting and reverting exposition on the beauty of the anointing. I highly recommend it for everyone in pursuit of God and His anointing.

Memory Mwangoh
Assistant Pastor, PAOZ-Upper Room Ministries, Harare, Zimbabwe.

Filled with thoughtful insights, Bishop Dambaza's new book *How To Receive And Release The Anointing* reveals the hidden truths that will cause you to desire the anointing of the Holy Spirit in a deeper way and how to release the anointing for the good and benefit of other people.

Watson Chitate
Home Care Groups and Outreach Pastor, PAOZ- Upper Room Ministries, Harare, Zimbabwe.

I have no doubt that the content in this book will help you have a deeper understanding of the anointing of God. Over the years, Bishop Dambaza has experienced God's anointing and God has used him in amazing ways to touch the lives of many people including here in the USA where he has ministered the Word of God on many occasions. I highly recommend this book to anyone who is genuinely thirsty and hungry for a fresh impartation of the Holy Spirit.

Peter Tembo
Lead Pastor,Christ Celebration Ministries, Teaneck, NJ, USA.

www.cccministries.info

It is with great joy I read the entire book written by my good friend and co-laborer in the gospel, Bishop Dambaza. The feeling of excitement in my spirit overwhelmed by the teaching of how to receive and release the anointing was so great. Anyone who feels the call of the Lord Jesus to witness and preach the gospel needs to realize the importance of depending on the anointing of the Holy Spirit for effective ministry.

This book is important for our generation when some people are just following gimmicks instead of the true anointing of God. One of the devastating facts and grievous errors of this generation is our fast pace which leaves no time to seek the true anointing that comes from God. Some ministers are often in a hurry to grow mega ministries not based on the solid foundation of the Word of God, but on the schemes of man and manipulation of false prophetic anointing that is presented as coming from God.

How To Receive And Release The Anointing will teach you to walk in the discipline of the Holy Spirit and receive what is from God and not from man. You will be able to learn the importance and the benefits of the anointing. You will also learn how you can receive the impartation of the anointing of the Holy Spirit. I strongly believe and pray that as you read this book your life will be challenged to dare to do great exploits for the sake of God's kingdom.

This book contains the anointing that is inherent in the Word of God. With the supernatural in origin, the eternal in duration, and the power of our Lord Jesus Christ that is inexpressible in value and infinite in scope, I challenge you to read this book with a receptive attitude.

When you read this book with the mentioned attitudes, you will tap into the regenerative power of the Holy Spirit and infallible authority of Almighty God. You will receive the impartation of the power from on high.

Please read this book and download the facts on how to receive and release the anointing of the Holy Spirit. I pray that you will enjoy reading this book and be challenged as much as I was challenged.

Dr. David Shamenda
Senior Pastor, Home City Church, Buffalo, NY, USA.

www.homecitychurch.com

The difference in achievement between high performers and those who struggle to make things happen in their lives can be traced to whether the people move in the supernatural power of God. In the absence of the anointing for your purpose and mission on earth, life becomes a struggle. It is like being given a knife to cut a huge baobab tree.

Berry Dambaza has unleashed the right tool fit for the work that each and every one of us has while walking on this earth which is to fulfil God's mandate in our lives. It is a known fact that fish will not exist for several minutes outside water but when it is in that sphere of influence, there is high productivity, fulfilment, passion and above all life itself.

It is however sad that as Christians we sometimes pay lip service to operating in the anointing of God and therefore at times feel ill-equipped to face the world and the multiplicity of challenges it brings. In this book, you will not only know what the anointing is all about, but you will also know how to receive and release the anointing.

This is a practical book. It pushes you towards action as well as removing any misconceptions you may have carried throughout your life on this very subject. Berry Dambaza gives live examples of his own journey in the Lord, impartations he received along the way to where he is today.

You cannot read this book and walk away the same. A shift is coming your way to the point that you receive and release the anointing to benefit others. I totally recommend this book.

Rabison Shumba
Author, Speaker, Coach, Business Strategist and Social
Entrepreneur, Harare, Zimbabwe.

www.rabisonshumba.com

I consider Bishop Berry Dambaza to be among anointed servants of God in the church today. It is a joy to wholeheartedly endorse this book of godly wisdom, biblical inspiration and practical experience showing us how to receive and release the anointing. I strongly believe that every believer and every minister of the gospel should read this book!

Funny Dube
PAOZ Harare Central Provincial Overseer and Senior Pastor of PAOZ- Fountain of
Hope Fellowship, Harare, Zimbabwe.

Holding this book in your hands, *How to Receive and Release the Anointing* by Bishop Berry Dambaza resembles a baton placed in the hand of the final runner in a four by four relay! Everyone knows what is at stake.

But by the time you are done reading this book you are going to realize that you are actually the baton and not the Runner and the Holy Spirit in you is that final Runner who guarantees you and I first place victory!!!

Cainos Manyara
Evangelist, Speaker and President, Founder and Senior Pastor of Omaha Dream Centre, NE, USA.

www.thismission.org

How To Receive and Release the Anointing by Bishop Berry Dambaza is an easy-to-read, uniquely captivating and all revealing classic among classics that I have ever read in recent times on the anointing. I highly recommend it.

Ronald Tebulu
Bishop and also the Senior Pastor, Evangel of Grace Church (PAOGZ), Monze, Zambia.

This compelling but straight forward book connects very well with Bishop Dambaza's first book entitled *How to Become A Vessel That God Can Use* in the practical ways in which it moves the believer from basic principles to higher levels where they can begin to do exploits in the kingdom of God. All this is made possible by the anointing that Bishop Berry Dambaza elucidates in this book.

Rolyn Mukudu
Director of Intercession Ministry, PAOZ-Upper Room Ministries, Harare, Zimbabwe.

This book will transform you and your ministry in a remarkable way. Bishop Dambaza simplifies this oft misunderstood subject in a way that can only be attributed to his personal experience and scriptural understanding of the anointing.

William Sibanda
Zone 1 Pastor, PAOZ-Upper Room Ministries, Harare, Zimbabwe.

Do you feel paralyzed, helpless and immobilized by fear? Do you desire the manifestation and Presence of God in your life? Bishop Dambaza's book prescribes for you the keys that will revitalize you and give you victory over fear and unleash the power of God's anointing in your life. The writer is a living testimony of the biblical principles contained in this powerful book

Joe Mundamawo
(MA in Leadership and management), Senior Pastor Holy Trinity Church, Harare.

Berry Dambaza is a unique man of God, a powerhouse preacher who knows the assignment on his life. What makes him unique however is his deep humility. As a result, he never competes with his peers but is always preferring them and willing to give them the platform first. I have watched him throughout the years consistently release spiritual sons and spiritual daughters that God has given him to live in their assignment and dreams.

Berry Dambaza is not building with himself in mind. He is living to ensure that his end is the next generation's beginning. For me, this is a huge part of his legacy that will speak long after his days have finished on this planet.

In this book Berry Dambaza defines what the anointing of God is from the start by stating that "The anointing is actually the ministering or serving grace that God lavishes upon us so that we can carry out the specific assignments that He Has given each of us." He is very direct about the need to live godly lives, teaching us that when our character is in line with God- "The anointing guarantees you success."

This book is filled with personal stories from a lifetime of ministry and will take you on an explorative journey of how the anointing impacted the heroes of scripture. There is an impartation for those who read the words on the pages of this book and it will "Turn ordinary people into extraordinary people!" Get ready to receive a fresh anointing as you read this book! One, two, three, four- Go!!!

Anthony Daley
Senior Pastor of the multi campus church, The Tabernacle in Clarksville and Indian Mound, TN, USA. TheTabernacle.us

Bishop Dambaza is a very experienced minister, anointed and gifted in the ministration of the Holy Spirit. His ministry is a clear testimony to that fact. Therefore he is qualified to teach on the anointing. In this book as a master, he skilfully articulates the mystery of impartation, a pivotal truth not taught by many preachers today yet it makes a great difference in who we become in life and ministry. I highly recommend this book to people who desire to be truly anointed of God and make a positive difference in this world. We have adapted this book as a text book for our School of Ministry.

Maxwell Cedric
Bishop, Redemption Faith Ministries International, Harare, Zimbabwe.

In this life we face inward and outward battles and wars. In order to really win these battles and wars, one has to practically win them in the spirit realm first. The anointing is the key and that divine enablement which makes one a winner. It is about a need for God to equip you in your daily endeavours that has led Bishop Dambaza to put on paper such a pool of wealth on the subject of the anointing.

This great wealth is a result of many years of experience, revelation, and knowledge which will impact your life for victory. Anyone who is hungry for spiritual empowerment and impartation has to read this book.

Bekezela Ndlovu
Apostle and Senior Pastor of Kingdom Life International Church-(KLIC) Bulawayo,
Zimbabwe.

Contents

Dedication

I dedicate this book to Dr. David A Newberry and Bishop Stephen Mwale whose lives and ministries have had a very big and positive impact upon my life and ministry.

Acknowledgements

I would like to acknowledge the following people:

- Bishop T. E. C. Manhanga, the Presiding Bishop of the PAOZ for his visionary leadership and spiritual covering. Your work ethic is a great inspiration to me and may the good Lord God Almighty bless you for the many times that you have worked beyond the call of duty and for your visionary and principalled leadership.
- Dr. James Seymour- Thank you for your leadership and the lessons you taught us at the Pentecostal Bible College on leadership and Homiletics and your love for the continent of Africa. At one time Africa was known as a dark continent. But through people like you, the light of the gospel is by the grace of God shining from the continent of Africa to the rest of the world with an ever increasing intensity.
- Pastor Chemani S. Tuturu of Harvest House International City Church, Harare- Thank you for finding the time from your busy schedule to thoroughly go through the manuscript, and for giving it a good layout as well as for the valuable suggestions that you gave me. You have inspired me a great deal in the area of writing through the many books that you wrote in a short space of time.
- Dr. A. T. Makoni-I thank you for your invaluable critique of the manuscript, your advice on some of the Greek words used in this book and for penning the foreword

to this book. You are a great inspiration to me and may the Lord use you mightily in this new and exciting season of your life.

- Pastor Carol Wasterfall of Parktown Pentecostal Church-Thank you for your encouragement.
- Mrs. Anne Mude-Thank you for the excellent work that you put into the manuscript and also for your willingness to go the extra mile.
- Mrs. Alletha Rukwata-Thank you for your vital assistance.
- Sister Ropafadzo Maphimidze- Thank you for your excellent editorial work.
- The PAOZ Family and in particular the PAOZ-Upper Room Ministries members and adherents including those scattered around the world-Thank you for your prayers, support, love and kindness. You mean the world to me and I love you all!

Foreword

It is truly humbling to foreword for this excellent treatment of a topical subject by the reputable servant of Christ, Bishop Berry Dambaza. It has always been a principle of biblical truth that a minister should be an embodiment of his message.

Having observed and followed Bishop Dambaza from a distance over the years I can honestly attest to the fact that within this manuscript, he is teaching what he practices. Many people seek to live what they preach rather than preach what they live.

Bishop Dambaza is a humble servant of God who has effectively and faithfully served the Lord and the Church of Jesus Christ. What he writes in this book emanates from practical experience in operating in the anointing of God.

There are many shooting stars today in the Body of Christ whose lights shine dazzlingly bright for a season and then quickly vanish, and fewer North stars which are consistent, durable and direction-setting. Bishop Dambaza is a North Star.

This publication is timely as it addresses a topic that has at times been abused and misrepresented. At last here is a balanced and biblical treatment of the subject. I highly recommend this offering as I believe that it will add value to believers across Africa and indeed around the world.

The New Testament is clear in teaching that all believers have the anointing because the Holy Spirit lives in them. However the anointing can be increased and stewarded so that it is administered more effectively. This is the thrust of this publication.

The emphasis that holiness, purity and integrity are essential to continue walking in the anointing is both biblical and welcome. I should add that since the anointing is given by the Holy Spirit as He wills as well as being granted to every believer, the anointing is not a proof of God's endorsement in terms of the preacher's behavior and lifestyle.

Some believers and ministers have walked in impurity and seemed for a season to walk in the anointing which led many to believe that the anointing is a sign of spirituality or divine endorsement. It is not necessarily so. The Corinthian Church manifested the gifts of the Spirit and yet seems to have been the most carnal of the New Testament churches.

Bishop Dambaza's teaching on "Beware of Merchandising the Anointing!" is on point. There are many in these last days who are unethically commercializing the anointing of God for profit. This is why Peter's admonition to the elders in 1 Peter 5:2 should be taken heed of. Shepherd the flock of God that is among you, exercising oversight, not under compulsion, but willingly, as God would have you; not for shameful gain, but eagerly" (English Standard Version)

There are also some who are trafficking in demonic anointing while claiming to be servants of Christ. There are two types of anointing namely an anointing from God and an anointing from the demonic world. The anointing of God is holy, pure and constructive. The demonic anointing is deceptive, destructive and dirty.

Many assume that all anointing is from God and therefore get deceived in the process. I highly recommend this offering to believers and to the Body of Christ so that we may walk in the anointing of God and proclaim the Gospel in the unction of the Holy Ghost with signs following as we anticipate the soon return of our Great God and Savior Jesus Christ.

Thank you Bishop Dambaza, for a clear and solid biblical treatment of this vital area of ministry. You are a great blessing and may your influence be felt past your own generation.

Dr. T. A. Makoni
(Author, Coach and Teaching Pastor)
Celebration Church,Borrowdale,Harare,Zimbabwe
www.nurturingchampios.com

Preface

How To Receive And Release The Anointing is a natural sequel to my first book, *How To Become A Vessel That God Can Use.* The anointing is a very necessary incredient to all who desire to be used by the Lord.

The thrust of this book is to reveal how one can receive the anointing and how one can release the anointing for the good and benefit of other people.

One of the pivotal truths that I share in this book is impartation. I strongly believe that impartation is a truth that we must understand for us to experience deeper realms of the anointing.

The role that music at times plays in the receiving and releasing of the anointing is one of truths we must get a grip on.

Beware of Merchandising the Anointing! Is the last chapter where I highlight some of the abuses of the anointing that we will do well to avoid. Here a few case studies drawn from the lives of Gehazi, Simon the sorcerer and Ananias and Sapphira present us with sober warnings concerning the abuse and misuse of the anointing.

Due to some of these abuses, some people have ended up avoiding this area of the anointing altogether! Just because someone drawned in a river does not necessarily mean stop drinking water! In spite of all the abuses that have happened in the area of the anointing, we must still seek to effectively flow in the anointing because we can never be really effective without the anointing!

I wrote this book to help all those with a deep desire to flow in the anointing to practically realise their dreams. That is why I have included some practical examples from my own life and ministry so that you can apply the truths contained in this book in your own life and ministry.

I strongly believe that God wants to use ordinary people in extraordinary ways. May this world be a better place because you dared to receive and release the anointing for the good and benefit of other people!

Bishop Berry Dambaza

Chapter One

WHAT IS THE ANOINTING?

1. What is The Meaning Of The Word "Anointing"?

The key root Greek words that speak of the anointing are as follows:

I. Chrio (to anoint) which means;

1. *To smear or rub with oil in order to consecrate for office or religious service.*
2. *Consecrating Jesus to the messianic office, and furnishing Him with the necessary powers for its administration.*
3. *Enduing Christians with gifts of the Holy Spirit.* (Thayer)

II. Aleipho (to anoint) which means;

1. *To rub or smear olive oil on the body.*
2. *Anointing brought for physical healing and relief and hence became synonymous with gladness (festivity).*
3. *To apply olive oil on the face, to refresh a guest. Oil was also applied to the feet to soothe and show honour (courtesy, respect). Anointing shares a "penetrating comfort" to impart strength and healing (joy).218 (Strong's Concordance)*

Jesus Christ is the Messiah which literally means the "**The Anointed One**". This title speaks of someone who is a king or high priest or liberator who is traditionally anointed with holy anointing oil.

In Hebrew "**Mashiach**" (Anointed), was a man who will be chosen by God to put an end to all the evil in the world, rebuild the temple and bring all the exiles back to Israel and usher in the world to come. It is better to use the Hebrew term Mashiach when speaking of the Jewish Messiah, because the Jewish concept is very different from the Christian one.

In Judaism this spoke of the awaited redeemer of the Jews, to be sent by God to free them. This usually speaks of Jesus Christ when regarded in this role.

In government, politics and diplomacy this speaks of an exceptional or hoped for liberator of a country or people. (Rich)

The Merriam Webster Dictionary definition of the word anoint is

1. To smear or rub with oil or an oily substance.
2. To apply oil as part of a religious ceremony. The priest anointed the sick.
3. To choose by or as if by divine election. Anoint him as his successor, also; to designate as if by a ritual anointment. Critics have anointed her as an important literary figure. (Merriam-Webster Dictionary)

*The woman saith unto Him, I know that **Messias** cometh, which is called Christ: when He is come, He will tell us all things. Jesus saith unto her, I that speak unto thee am He. (John 4:25)KJV*

*He first findeth his own brother Simon, and he saith unto him,We have found the **Messias**, which is, being interpreted, the Christ. (John 1:41) KJV*

The Lord Jesus Christ outlined His assignment when He had these words concerning Himself read the scriptures;

*"The Spirit of the Lord is upon me, because He Hath **anointed me***

1. *To preach the gospel to the poor;*
2. *He hath **sent me to heal the brokenhearted**,*
3. *To preach deliverance to the captives, and*
4. *Recovering of the sight to the blind,*
5. *To set at liberty them that are bruised,*
6. *To preach the acceptable year of the Lord." (Luke 4:18, 19)KJV*

I have deliberately put the scriptures above in point form for us to clearly see the purposes of the anointing that was upon the Lord Jesus Christ.

The anointing is actually the ministering or serving grace that God lavishes upon us so that we can carry out the specific assignments that He Has given each of us.

Apostle Nahum Rosario in His book entitled *The Secrets of the Anointing* defines the anointing in this way: *"We can say that the anointing is the method of operation for the Spirit of God here on earth. It involves all the graces, abilities, and powers that the Spirit concedes to us in order for us to perform the works of God and meet the spiritual needs of humanity"* (Nahum).

Apostle Guillermo Maldonado in his book *How to walk in the supernatural power of God* describes the anointing in this way; *"Since the coming of the Holy Spirit in the New Testament, the anointing has generally been the ability God gives the believer to accomplish the work of ministering in His name and serving Him."* (Maldonado)

2. Other Synonymous Terms For The Anointing

The anointing has several synonymous Biblical terms by which it is known. Here are some of them:

1. **The Enduement Of Power**: (Luke 24:29; Acts 1:8)KJV
2. **Being Filled With The Holy Ghost**: (Acts 2:4; Acts 4:31; Ephesians 4:18)KJV
3. **Receiving The Holy Ghost**: (Acts 2:38; Acts 19:2; Acts 10:47; Acts 8:15)KJV
4. **Being Baptized In The Holy Ghost**: (Matthew 3:11; Acts 1:5; Mark 1:8)KJV
5. **The Outpouring Of The Holy Spirit**: (Acts 2:17; Acts 10:45; Joel 2:28-29)KJV
6. **The Power Of The Lord:**(Luke 5:17)KJV
7. **Virtue Or Power**: *(*Mark 5:30; Luke 6:19; Luke 8:46;Acts 4:33)KJV
8. **Gift**:(1Peter 4:10; Romans 12:6; 1 Timothy 4:14; 2Timothy 1:6)KJV
9. **Grace**: (Ephesians 4:7; Romans 12:6; Galatians 2:9;1Corinthians 15:10)KJV

10. Gift Of The Grace Of God:(Ephesians 3:7;1Peter 4:10)KJV
11. Divine Ability Or Divine Enablement:(1Peter 4:10)KJV

This list is by no means exhaustive because there are still many other synonymous Biblical terms that I have not mentioned here.

3. The Anointing Separates One For Holy Purposes

The articles in the tabernacle were **consecrated**, **sanctified** or **set apart for God's service** by anointing them with the holy anointing oil.

Exodus 30:26-29(KJV)

*26. And thou shalt **anoint** the tabernacle of the congregation therewith, and the ark of the testimony,*

27. And the table and all his vessels, and the candlestick and his vessels, and the altar of incense,

28. And the altar of burnt offering with all his vessels, and the laver and his foot.

*29. And thou shalt **sanctify them, that they may be most holy: whatsoever toucheth them shall be holy**.*

In the same way that every vessel in the temple was set apart or sanctified for holy use and service, someone is set apart for sacred service when anointed with the holy anointing oil.

Priests were anointed and set apart to minister in their functions.

Therefore the anointing signifies divine appointment,empowering,placement and the authority to carry out God's assignment.

*And thou shalt **anoint** Aaron and His sons, and **consecrate them**, that they may **minister unto me in the priest's office**. (Exodus 30:30)KJV*

God held the exclusive right as to who got anointed. No one was allowed to just wake up one day, make the holy anointing oil and take that anointing oil and pour it on someone! Anyone who dared to disobey this instruction did it at the peril of their own life!

*Whosoever compoundeth any like it (the holy anointing oil), or whosoever putteth any of it upon a stranger, shall even **be cut off** from His people. (Exodus 30:33)KJV*

Saving Grace

I am sure we are all familiar with the saving grace by which we have received our salvation. ***For by grace are ye saved through faith**; and that not of yourselves: it is the gift of God: Not of works, lest any man should boast. (Ephesians 2:8, 9)KJV*

The wages of sin is death; but the gift of God is eternal life through Jesus Christ our Lord. (Romans 6:23)KJV

***Who hath saved us**, **and called us with an holy calling**, not according to our works, but according to His own purpose and grace, which was given us in Christ Jesus before the world began. (2Timothy1:9)KJV*

It is important to realise that the word grace does not only refer to the saving grace but at times it refers to the serving or ministering grace which is the anointing.

The *saving grace* separates us from the world unto the Lord so that the *serving* or *ministering* grace which is the anointing can empower us to serve the Lord in whatever area the Lord assigns us. In the saving grace we are *sealed with that Holy Spirit of promise (Ephesians 1:13)KJV*

Serving Grace

*"…If any man **minister,**let him do it as of **the ability which God giveth**…"(1 Peter 4:11) KJV* The ability which God gives is the anointing.

This verse is preceded by this verse: *As every man hath **received the gift**, even so **minister** the same to one another, as good stewards of the manifold(many faceted) **grace of God.**(1Peter4:10)KJV* God's grace is multifaceted.

*But **by the grace of God** I am what I am: and **His grace** which was bestowed upon me was not in vain; but I labored more abundantly than they all: yet not I, **but the grace of God** which was with me. (1 Corinthians 15:10)KJV*

***Where of I was made a minister**, according to the gift of the grace of God given unto me **by the effectual working of His power.** (Ephesians 3:7)KJV*

The grace spoken of in these preceding verses is the ***serving,enabling,empowering or ministering grace**(which is the anointing).*

*And with **<u>great power</u>** gave the apostles witness of the resurrection of the Lord Jesus: and **<u>great grace</u>** was upon them all.(Acts 4:33)KJV* It is very apparent that this verse is referring to the anointing that enabled the apostles to preach the gospel with **great power** or **great grace**. These two terms are speaking of the same thing and that thing is the anointing.

Beyond these two facets of grace that I have mentioned, (the **saving grace** and the **serving grace**), there are other facets of grace. For example there is:

1. **The grace of giving**(2Corintians 8:1-5)KJV
2. **The grace of life**(1Peter 3:7)KJV
3. **Calling** which is **by the grace of God**(Galatians 1:15)KJV
4. Paul was given **the grace to preach** to the Gentiles(Galatians 2:9)KJV
5. The **empowering or strengthening grace**(2 Corinthians 12:9)KJV

I could go on enumerating the many other facets of grace. However, my focus of teaching in this book is on the serving, ministering, enabling or empowering grace which is the anointing.

3. The Person Of The Holy Spirit Is The Reality Behind Anointing!

*Then Samuel took the horn of oil, and **anointed** him in the midst of his brethren: and **the Spirit of the Lord came upon David from that day forward**. So Samuel rose up, and went to Ramah.*(1 Samuel 16:13)KJV

While symbols like **oil**, **a dove**, **water**, **a seal**, **fire**, **wind**, **a cloud**, etc., may indeed be shadows, types, and symbols of the Holy Spirit, *the Holy Spirit is definitely not any of these elements!* **The reality behind all these shadows, types and symbols of the Holy Spirit is the Holy Spirit.**

This fact goes beyond all the shadows, types and symbols of the anointing lest we hold on to these things and miss out on the reality of the person of the Holy Spirit! It seems man has a high propensity to gravitate towards shadows,types,and symbols instead of the Living God.

Personal Traits of The Holy Spirit

1. The Holy Spirit is able to express **emotions** or **feelings**. He can be grieved. That is why the Bible says, *"Grieve not the Holy Spirit of God" (Ephesians 4:30)KJV*
2. The Holy Spirit Has a **mind** or in other words He is capable of thinking. *And He that searcheth the hearts knoweth what is the **mind** of the (Holy)Spirit.(Romans 8:27)KJV*
3. The Holy Spirit Has a will through which He expresses His power of choice. *But all these worketh that one and the selfsame Spirit, dividing to every man severally as He **will**. (1Corinthians 12:11)KJV*

There is therefore a greater need for us to develop a closer relationship with the Holy Spirit. The closer our relationship with the Holy Spirit becomes, the greater the anointing that flows upon us and through us.

*Or do you suppose that the scripture is speaking to no purpose when it says, The Spirit whom He has caused to dwell in us yearns over us- and He yearns for the Spirit [**to be welcome**]-with jealous love? James 4:5 (Amplified Bible, Classic Edition) AMPC*

The Holy Spirit does not feel welcome in our lives when we treat Him like an impersonal thing that has no feelings, capacity to think and the power of choice.

Oh, how He longs to fellowship or commune with us! That is why the Word of God says, *"The grace of the Lord Jesus Christ, and the love of God, and **the communion of the Holy Ghost, be with you all**.Amen."(2 Corinthians 13:14)KJV* The communion or fellowship of the Holy Spirit is supposed to be an experience for **all** believers. The Lord Jesus Christ said, *"But if I go away, I will send Him(The Holy Spirit) to you-**to be in close fellowship with you**." John16:7 (Amplified Bible, Classic Edition) AMPC*.

Are you in close fellowship with the Holy Spirit or you have totally ignored Him?

*But **the anointing** which ye have received of Him abideth in you, and ye need not that any man teach you: but as **the same anointing teacheth you of all things**, and is truth, and is no lie, ye shall abide in Him.(1John 2:27)KJV* Here the anointing is clearly shown as a person capable of teaching us all things. An impersonal thing would not possess that kind of ability.

The Holy Spirit desires to commune or fellowship with each one of us. He is a personal divine being not just an impersonal raw power at our disposal and control.We must learn to yield to the Holy Spirit lest we end up thinking that we can use the Holy Spirit for our own ends and whims.

CONCLUSION

Allow the Holy Spirit to flow through you as He desires without anyhindrance from you. Fully surrender to Him.

God is not looking for your ability but your availability so that *He can display His ability or anointing through you.*

*"…If any man **minister,**let him do it as of **the ability**(or the anointing)**which God giveth**…"(1 Peter 4:11)KJV*

The anointing gives you the divine ability to minister to other people

Chapter Two

BENEFITS OF THE ANOINTING

What are the benefits of the anointing? What do we profit or gain from the anointing? *Here are some of the benefits of the anointing:*

1. The Anointing Gives You Purpose

One of the most powerful benefits of the anointing is that the anointing gives you a revelation of your purpose. The late Myles Munroe said,

"Everything has a purpose but not all purpose is known and when purpose is not known abuse is inevitable (Excellent)"

You are wired for something in this life and that something is your God-given purpose.

And thou shalt put upon Aaron the holy garments, and anoint him; that he may minister unto me in the priest's office.(Exodus 40:13)KJV

The anointing that was administered upon Aaron clearly gave him his purpose which was to minister in the priest's office.

Do you know your purpose in life? If you don't know you can know your purpose through the anointing!

The *"Anointing teacheth you all things" (1John 2:27)KJV The "all things'* here includes your purpose in life. It is again the late Myles Munroe who said that *"The greatest tragedy in life is not death, but a life without a purpose* (Pinterest)"

God has a purpose for your life. Unless you walk in God's purpose for your life, you will live an unfulfilled life!

When you do not know what your life's purpose is, it is easy to abuse your life and waste time and be of no use to those you are supposed to be useful to.

There are people who are living outside God's purpose for their lives. You don't have to be among such people because the anointing gives you the revelation of your purpose.

2. The Anointing Brings God's Power Into Your Life

*How God anointed Jesus of Nazareth with the Holy Ghost and with **power**: who went about doing good, and healing all that were oppressed of the devil; for God was with him. (Acts 10:38)KJV*

Christ was anointed with the Holy Ghost and with power. **That power enabled Him to do His ministry with effective results.**

*For the kingdom of God is not in **Word** only,but in **power**.(1 Corinthians 4:20)KJV*

*For our gospel came not unto you in **Word** only,but also in **power,** and in the **Holy Ghost**, and in much assurance; as ye know what manner of men we were among you for your sake. (1Thessalonians 1:5)KJV*

Who will display the power of God to your generation if not you? If not now,then when?

*And my speech and my preaching was not with enticing words of man's wisdom, but in demonstration of the **Spirit** and of **power**:That your faith should not stand in the wisdom of men, **but in the power of God.**(1 Corinthians 2:4)KJV*

It is time to go beyond mere speech and demonstrate the power of the living God to our own generation!

Whatever the Lord has purposed for your life, you need the power of God to be effective.

Exodus 35:30-33(KJV)

30. And Moses said unto the children of Israel; see, the LORD hath called by name Bezaleel the son of Uri, the son of Hur, of the tribe of Judah;

*31. And hath filled him with the **Spirit of God,** in **wisdom,** in **understanding,** and in **knowledge,** and in **all manner of workmanship;***

32. And to devise curious works, to work in gold, and in silver, and in brass,

33. And in cutting stones, to set them, and in cutting wood, and to make any manner of cunning work.

Here the Lord filled Bezaleel and his company with the Spirit of God which is the anointing. That is what gave Bezaleel and his counterparts the power to do all manner of expert workmanship.

We need the anointing to operate effectively in every sector of our communities. Do not restrict the anointing to spiritual matters only because the anointing is relevant for every area of our lives like sports,art,industry,economics,science,politics,education,health, etc.

3. The Anointing Brings The Manifestation Of The Presence of God

*How God anointed Jesus Christ of Nazareth with the Holy Ghost and with power: who went about doing good, and healing all that were oppressed of the devil; **for God was with Him!**(Acts 10:38)KJV*

The anointing brings the manifestation of the Presence of God. No one can argue with the Presence of God.

It is the Presence of God that makes a positive difference in our lives and ministries.

*The same came to Jesus by night, and said unto Him, Rabbi, we know that thou art a teacher come from God: **for no man can do these miracles that thou doest, except God be with Him.**(John 3:2)KJV*

We must allow the Presence of God to powerfully manifest in our lives through the anointing. Nicodemus perceived the presence of God in the life and ministry of the Lord Jesus Christ.

*Ye men of Israel hear these words; Jesus of Nazareth, a man approved of God among you by miracles and wonders and signs, **which God did by Him** in the midst of you, as ye yourselves also know.(Acts 2:22)KJV*

4. The Anointing Brings Revelations Of The Things Of God Into Our Lives

Now we have received, not the spirit of the world, but the Spirit which is of God; that we might know the things that are freely given to us of God.(1 Corinthians 2:12)KJV

1 Corinthians 2:9, 10(KJV

9. But as it is written, Eye hath not seen, nor ear heard, neither have entered into the heart of man, the things which God hath prepared for them that love him.

10. But God hath revealed them unto us by His Spirit: for the Spirit searcheth all things, yea, the deep things of God.

It is the anointing that gives us insight into the things of God,even the deep things of God.

John 16:13, 14(KJV)

13.Howbeit when He, the Spirit of truth, is come, He will guide you into all truth: for He shall not speak of Himself; but whatsoever He shall hear, that shall He speak: and He will shew you things to come.

14. He shall glorify me: for He shall receive of mine, and shall shew it unto you.

That is the reason Paul prayed for the Ephesians in this manner:

Ephesians 1:17-19(KJV)

17.That the God of our Lord Jesus Christ, the Father of glory, may give unto you the spirit of wisdom and revelation in the knowledge of Him,

18. The eyes of your understanding being enlightened; that ye may know what the hope of His calling, and what the riches of the glory of his inheritance in the saints.

19. And what is the exceeding greatnessof His power to us-ward who believe, according to the working of His mighty power.

5. The Anointing Brings Divine Protection

The Lord is their strength, and He is the saving strength of His anointed.(Psalm 28:8)KJV

Psalm 20:6-7(KJV)

6. Now know I that the Lord saveth His anointed; He will hear him from His holy heaven with the saving strength of His right hand.

7. Some trust in chariots, and some in horses: but we will remember the name of the Lord our God.

He suffered no man to do them wrong: yea, He reproved kings for their sakes; Saying, Touch not mine anointed, and do my prophets no harm. (Psalm 105:14-15)KJV

Some years ago I was involved in an automobile accident. The vehicle that I was driving was hit on the front side and backside and dragged for some distance. I sustained no injuries and came out of the wreckage intact.

After my wife came out of the vehicle she collapsed and fainted but was revived after water was poured over her body. She had no injuries. In fact if she had not been wearing the seat belt she could have been thrown out of the vehicle through the front windscreen! Of course that would have been tragic!

Other passengers who were in the vehicle came out of the vehicle with no injuries save one with a minor injury. Had it not been for the Lord's protection, we would have all perished in that accident because the vehicle was badly damaged. People who saw the damaged vehicle wondered how we came out alive.

Nothing evil can touch you unless the Lord permits. Sometimes the Lord permits certain things to happen in our lives because of His purposes. For instance the tragic events that happened in the life of Job were permitted by the Lord. They could not have happened had the Lord not permitted the devil to go ahead and touch Job, his children and his substance. (Job 1:12-22)KJV

Hast not thou made an hedge about him, and about his house, and about all that he hath on every side? Thou hast blessed the work of his hands, and his substance is increased in the land.(Job1:10)KJV These are the words that the devil spoke concerning Job. He clearly acknowledged that there was a protective hedge around Job and he could not harm Job because of that hedge.

That protective hedge speaks of the anointing. The devil could not penetrate that hedge of protection without the Lord's permission.

Even the death of our Lord Jesus Christ together with the persecution He faced prior to His death were things that the Lord permitted to happen because of His own divine purposes.

1 Corinthians 2:7, 8(KJV)
7. Howbeit we speak wisdom among them that are perfect: yet not the wisdom of this world, nor of the princes of this world that came to nought:
8. Which none of the princes of this world knew: for had they known it, they would not have crucified the Lord of glory.
Acts 4:27, 28KJV)
27. For a truth against thy holy child Jesus, whom thou Hast anointed, both Herod, and Pontius Pilate, with the Gentiles, and the people of Israel, were gathered together.
28. For to do whatsoever thy hand and thy counsel determined to be done.

Whatever they did to the Lord Jesus Christ was permitted by the Lord God Almighty and actually brought salvation to mankind. Had the princes of this world known that this would bring salvation to mankind, they would have not crucified the Lord of glory!

6. The Anointing Will Transform You

1 Samuel 10:6-7(KJV)

*6. And the **Spirit of the LORD** will come upon thee, and thou shalt prophesy with them, and **thou shalt be turned into another man.***

7. And let it be, when these signs are come unto thee, that thou do as occasion serves thee; for God is with thee.

The anointing transformed Saul into another man.

Matthew 26:69-75KJV)

69. Now Peter sat without in the palace: and a damsel came unto him, saying, Thou also wast with Jesus of Galilee.

*70. **But he denied before them all, saying, I know not what thou sayest:***

71. And when he was gone out into the porch, another maid saw him, and said unto them that they were there, This fellow was also with Jesus of Nazareth.

*72. **And again he denied with an oath, I do not know the man.***

73. And after a while came unto him they that stood by, and said to Peter, Surely thou also art one of them; for thy speech betrayeth thee.

*74. **Then began he to curse and to swear, saying, I know not the man.** And immediately the cock crew.*

*75. And Peter remembered the word of Jesus, which said unto him, Before the cock crows, thou shalt deny me thrice. **And he went out, and wept bitterly***

When Peter was confronted about his association with the Lord Jesus Christ he denied the Lord Jesus Christ thrice because of fear. But, oh, what a transformation he had when the anointing came upon him as depicted in the verses below:

Acts 4:8-10(KJV)

*8. Then Peter, filled with the **Holy Ghost,** said unto them, Ye rulers of the people, and elders of Israel,*

9. If we this day be examined of the good deed done to the impotent man, by what means he is made whole;

*10.**Be it known unto you all, and to all the people of Israel, that by the name of Jesus Christ of Nazareth, whom ye crucified, whom God raised from the dead, even by Him doth this man stand here before you whole.***

Acts 4:13-14(KJV)

*13. **Now when they saw the boldness of Peter and John**, and perceived that they were unlearned and ignorant men, **they marvelled;** and they took knowledge of them, that they had been with Jesus.*

14. And beholding the man which was healed standing with them, they could say nothing against it

The anointing turns ordinary people into extraordinary people! What you are able to accomplish through the anointing is beyond human power.

*But we have this treasure in jars of clay,to show that the surpassing **power** belongs **to God** and **not to us**.2Corinthians 4:7(English Standard Version) ESV.*

Let the operation of the exceeding greatness of of God's power be manifested in and through your life.

7. The Anointing Endues You with The Necessary Gifts of The Holy Spirit

*But it is God Who confirms and makes us steadfast and establishes us (in joint fellowship) with you in Christ, and Has consecrated and **anointed us-enduing us with the gifts of the Holy Spirit**. 1Corinthians 1:21 Amplified Bible Classic Edition (AMPC)*

*God also bearing them witness, both with signs and wonders, and with divers miracles, and **gifts of the Holy Ghost**, according to His own will? (Hebrews 2:4)KJV*

Whomsoever God calls He anoints and empowers with the necessary gifts of the Holy Spirit.

8. The Anointing Opens The Right Doors For You!

Isaiah 45:1-3(KJV)

*1.**Thus saith the Lord to His anointed,** to Cyrus, whose right hand I have holden, to subdue nations before him; and I will loose the loins of kings, to open before him the two leaved gates; and the gates shall not be shut;*

2.I will go before thee,and make the crooked places straight:I will break in pieces the gates of brass, and cut in sunder the bars of iron:

*3. And **I will give thee the treasures of darkness,** and **hidden riches of secret places,** that thou mayest know that I, the Lord, which call thee by thy name, am the God of Israel.*

If the Lord could do these things for Cyrus who did not even know the Lord, how much more will He do for you who know the Lord?

God cannot anoint you only for Him to fail to find a place for you to function! Anointed people do not function in a vacuum but where there are structures and He will put you in the right place.

*But now hath God set the members every one of them in the body, **as it Hath pleased Him.** (1Corinthians 12:18)KJV*

God sets members in the body as it pleases Him, not as it pleases you or please other people! The Lord goes before you to make crooked places straight and opening the right doors for you! These are powerful benefits of the anointing.

9. The Anointing Gives You Victory Over Fear

Fear thou not; for I am with thee: be not dismayed; for I am thy God: I will strengthen thee; yea, I will help thee; yea, I will uphold thee with the right hand of My righteousness. (Isaiah 41:10)KJV

For God hath not given us the spirit of fear; but of power, and of love, and of a sound mind.(2 Timothy 1:7)KJV

Many people are paralyzed and immobilized by fear. But the anointing gives you victory and mastery over fear.

The anointing gives you courage and confidence.

When Joshua took over the role of leading the Children of Israel from Moses, it was such a mammoth task for him. The Lord encouraged Joshua by telling him to be strong and courageous.

Be strong *and **of a good courage…Only be thou strong** and **very courageous…Be strong** and **of a good courage;be not afraid, neither be thou dismayed: for the LORD thy God is with thee whithersoever thou goest**. (Joshua 1:6, 7, 9)KJV*

If God is with you, there is no need to be afraid. *What shall we then say to these things? If God be for us, who can be against us? (Romans 8:31)KJV*

10. The Anointing Brings Healing And Deliverance

*How God **anointed** Jesus Christ of Nazareth with **the Holy Ghost** and with **power:** who went aboutdoing good,and **healing** all that were oppressed of the devil; for God was with him.(Acts 10:38)KJV*

*And they cast out many devils, and **anointed with oil** many that were sick, and healed them. (Mark 6:13)KJV*

The anointing endues you with the power to heal the sick and deliver those who are bound and oppressed by the devil.

*Then Philip went down to the city of Samaria, and preached Christ unto them. The people with one accord gave heed unto those things which Philip spake, hearing and seeing the miracles which he did. **For unclean spirits, crying with loud voice, came out of many that were possessed with them: and many taken with palsies, and that were lame, were healed. And there was great joy in that city.** (Acts 8:5-8)KJV*

Philip demonstrated the power of the gospel when he preached the gospel in Samaria. Besides hearing the Word of God, people saw the demonstration of God's healing and delivering power.

Acts 5:14-16(KJV)

14. And believers were the more added to the Lord, multitudes both of men and women.

15. Insomuch that they brought forth the sick into the streets, and laid them on beds and couches, that at the least the shadow of Peter passing by might overshadow some of them.

*16. There came also a multitude out of the cities round about unto Jerusalem, **bringing sick folks, and them which were vexed with unclean spirits: and they were healed everyone.***

If you are sick you can call upon the elders of the church so that they can pray for you and anoint you with oil according to the Word of God.

James 5:14,15(KJV)

*14. Is there any sick among you? Let him call for the elders of the church; and let them pray over him, **anointing him with oil** in the name of the Lord:*

15. And the prayer of faith shall save the sick, and the Lord shall raise him up; and if he have committed sins, they shall be forgiven him.

I have seen God heal many people through His anointing. In one of our Miracle Healing Services a lady came with a neck brace. She was in great pain.

I strongly felt led by the Lord to call her and pray for her. After praying for her I told her to take the neck brace off her neck and to begin to bend her neck sideways. She did what I said and was instantly healed and the pain that she had been feeling was completely gone!

I remember being led to pray for Mrs. Nyanguru in one of our Sunday services. She was having problems with her leg and was using a walking stick. The Lord touched her miraculously and she stopped using the walking stick.

Recently we had a conference in our branch church in Eskbank near the capital city. I was praying for people at the altar call when I had a word of knowledge and spoke out that word. I said there is a person who is feeling a headache and as I am speaking that headache is disappearing now.

Mrs. Violet Mukuku later testified that she had had a terrible headache that was bothering her. When that word was spoken she was instantly healed. There are many testimonies of healing that I can recount but due to space limitations I will stop here.

11. The Anointing Brings the Manifestation of Signs and Wonders

Romans 15:18-19(KJV)

18. For I will not dare to speak of any of those things which Christ hath not wrought by me, to make the Gentiles obedient, by Word and deed,

*19. **Through mighty signs and wonders, by the power of the Spirit of God;** so that from Jerusalem, and round about unto Illyricum, I have fully preached the gospel of Christ.*

Paul was successful in his life because of the manifestation of signs and wonders in his ministry. As children of God, God desires to use us in the dimension of miraculous signs and wonders.

*And by the hands of the apostles were **many signs** and **wonders** wrought among the people. (Acts 5:12)KJV*

Long time therefore abode they speaking boldly in the Lord, which gave testimony unto the Word of His grace, and granted **signs** *and* **wonders** *to be done by their hands.(Acts 14:3)KJV*

Operating in miracles,signs and wonders should be a normal thing for every born again-child of God. The great commission of the Lord Jesus Christ is a commission of signs and wonders.

Mark 16:15, 17-18(KJV)

15. Go ye into all the world, and preach the gospel to every creature.

17. And these signs shall follow them that believe;In my name shall they castout devils; they shall speak with new tongues;

18. They shall take up serpents; and if they drink any deadly thing, it shall not hurt them; they shall lay hands on the sick, and they shall recover.

CONCLUSION

Let us do our part and God will always be faithful to do His part. We must learn to do our part and see God at work in us and through us through His anointing.

And they went forth,and preached everywhere,the Lord **working** *with them, andconfirming The* **Word with signs following** *Amen.(Mark 16:20)KJV* Step out by faith on the Word of God. The Lord is ever ready to confirm His Word as *He watches over it to perform it.(Jeremiah 1:12)KJV*

The secret to experiencing the release of the anointing in your life is to do your natural part and expect God to do His supernatural part

Chapter Three

THE POWER OF IMPARTATION

What does to impart mean?

According to the digital Merriam Webster Dictionary, *to impart is;*

1. ***To give (something)**, such as quality to a thing.*
2. ***To make (something) known to someone.***

To impart also means **to conduct, convey, give, communicate, spread, transfer, transfuse, and transmit** according to the Merriam Webster Dictionary. (Merriam-webster Dictionary)

From the above descriptions, it is clear that ***impartation is the act of giving, transferring, transmitting or communicating something***. This very book that you are reading is imparting knowledge to you on how to receive and release the anointing.

Come to think of it, we all participate in the act of imparting or receiving something on a daily basis!

The **root Greek word** from which impartation is derived according to Biblesofts New Exhaustive Strong's Numbers and Concordance with Expanded Greek-Hebrew Dictionary is

Metadinomi NT: 3330 metadinomi (**met-ad--id'-o-mee**); from NT: 3326 and NT: 1325; *to giveover*, i.e. *share:* KJV-**give**, imparticiple. (Biblesoft)

*For I long to see you, that I may **impart** unto you some **spiritual gift**, to the end ye may be established.(Romans 1:11)KJV*

1. Impartation May Come Through Laying On Of Hands

One of the most common ways through which impartation of the anointing is transmitted is through the laying on of hands.

According to the Wikipedia *the laying on of hands is a ritual that is a part of religious practices found in various cultures throughout the world.*

In Christian churches, this practice is used as both a symbolic and formal method of invoking the Holy Spirit primarily during baptisms and confirmations, healing services, blessings, and ordination of priests, ministers, elders, deacons, and other church offices, along with a variety of other church sacraments and holy ceremonies.

*Wherefore I put thee in remembrance that thou stir up **the gift of God**, which is **in** thee **by the putting on of my hands**.(2 Timothy 1:6)KJV*

Through the laying on of hands, the gift (*or the anointing*) of God was imparted to Timothy. In other words, through the laying on of hands, there was an impartation of the anointing that was given to Timothy.

And in those days, when the number of the disciples was multiplied, there arose a murmuring of the Grecians against the Hebrews, because their widows were neglected in daily ministration.

(Acts 6:1)KJV

The disciples were asked by the apostles to choose seven honest men full of the Holy Ghost and wisdom among them whom they wished to appoint over this matter of daily ministration.

Acts6:6, 7(KJV)

*6. Whom they set before the apostles: and when they had prayed, **they laid their hands on them**.*

*7. And the **Word of God increased;** and the number of the disciples **multiplied in Jerusalem greatly;** and **a great company of the priests were obedient** to the faith.*

Tangible results were manifested through this act of laying on of hands as reflected in the preceding verses.

Acts 13:2, 3(KJV)

2. As they ministered to the Lord, and fasted, the Holy Ghost said, Separate me Barnabas and Saul for the work whereunto I have called them.

*3. And **when they had fasted and prayed, and laid their hands on them**, they sent them away.*

*And **when they had ordained them elders in every church**, and **had prayed with fasting**, they commended them to the Lord, on whom they had believed.(Acts 14:23)KJV* Although nothing here is said about the laying on of hands, it was a standard practice to do so on such occasions.

2. Impartation May Come Through Prophesy And The Laying On Of Hands

*Neglect not **the gift that is in thee**, **which was given thee by prophecy, with the laying on of the hands of the presbytery** (or the elders).(1Timothy 4:14)KJV*

Through prophesy and the laying on of hands impartation of the anointing can be transferred, transmitted and received. It is critically important to receive what is transferred, transmitted and released by faith.

Laying on of hands should not be done haphazardly but with great care and seriousness.

Do not be in a hurry in the laying on of hands *[giving the sanction of the church too quickly in reinstating expelled offenders or in ordination in questionable cases], nor participate in another man's sins; keep yourself pure. 1 Timothy 5:22 Amplified Bible Classic Edition (AMPC)*

3. Personal Encounters Of Impartation

When I got saved, Bishop Stephen Mwale became my pastor. I sat under his ministry for a period of approximately a year and four months. During that period I caught the anointing to preach the Word of God by constantly watching Bishop Stephen Mwale powerfully preach the Word of God.

That was during the period of 1980 to1981 in the city of Ndola, Zambia where as a family we were residing. I actually adopted his preaching style howbeit unconsciously!

According to Pastor DeAndre Patterson,*anointings are caught, not taught.*

I became instinctively aware that if I were to be given the opportunity to preach,I would have preached the Word of God with no problem whatsoever because I had received the impartation to preach the Word of God by watching Bishop Stephen Mwale preach the Word of God.

I started going into the woods close to where I lived and preached to the trees. I would even make altar calls and pray for the sick all by myself after preaching to the trees! In my mind I took the trees as my congregation!

Had some people seen me preaching to the trees, they would have thought that I had gone bananas!

This was the place where simulation occurred and through these stints,my preaching of the gospel immensely improved long before I ever preached to real people!

In 1984, Evangelist Reinhard Bonnke held a gospel crusade at Glammis Stadium at the Exhibition Park, then known as the Harare Agricultural Show Grounds.

I desperately wanted Evangelist Reinhard Bonnke to pray for me with the laying on of hands because of my deep belief in the power of impartation.

It was not easy to get him to do that with all the security and ushering team that shielded him. But I was determined to get to him in spite of those obstacles. I finally got to him at his caravan and told him my request.

He graciously laid his hands on me and prayed for me. It is through such encounters that I believe that some of the anointings that flow through me came upon me.

The way I usually minister the baptism in the Holy Spirit, where I encourage those seeking this experience to count one up to four and then shout hallelujah is something I learned through observing Evangelist Reinhard Bonnke!

And what I saw in Evangelist Reinhard Bonnke's meetings usually happens in some of the meetings I conduct, and we have witnessed many people receive the baptism in the Holy Spirit with the evidence of speaking in other tongues and sometimes with dramatic manifestations of the power of God.

Some of my protégés have since learned this from me and are doing exactly like I do as they minister the baptism in the Holy Spirit!

All I can say is that impartation is real and works if one dares to place a demand on the anointing!

In 1994 I attended a conference in Bulawayo hosted by Jesus Life Ministries International, headed by Evangelist Randy Close.

Evangelist Dr. David A. Newberry, who was one of the guest speakers at that conference, preached a powerful message and then called for an altar call.

Many people responded to that altar call, including myself. I was standing on the fringes of this group that responded to the altar call when Dr.David A. Newberry called my name and immediately started speaking a prophetic word over my life.

The essence of the prophetic word was that there was a seven-fold increase in the anointing that was coming upon my life.

The power of God came upon me and I fell down to the floor without anyone touching me.

When I returned home after the conference and preached the Word of God in my local church in Kambuzuma,Harare,there was such a great manifestation of God's power when I prayed for people.

Something had indeed happened to me! People were being touched by the power of God in ways that we were not accustomed to.

I was to meet Dr. A Newberry again in 1997, at the Action '97 Conference of Celebration Church, then known as Hear The Word Ministries in the foyer of the Harare International Conference Centre.

Dr. David A Newberry laid his hands on me after we had exchanged greetings, and I fell down under the power of God. Dr. David A Newberry proceeded to the main auditorium and left me laying on the floor!I of course later on managed to rise up and joined the service in the auditorium.

Impartation is a powerful spiritual reality that we must comprehend. It is an avenue through which we can receive the anointing that can make a positive difference in both our lives and ministries.

I was privileged to work under Dr. David A Newberry from 1985 to 1986 when he led an evangelistic ministry called Miracle Rain Crusades. We had people like Brother Ken Patel, Pastor Robert Westerfall, Pastor Samuel Ndove and Evangelist Randy Close in the team.

Dr. David A Newberry besides running this evangelistic ministry was principally working as a missionary of the Assemblies of God General Council (Zimbabwe).

It was through Miracle Rain Crusades that I had the privilege of proclaiming the Word of God to massive crowds during evangelistic campaigns. I remember in June 1986 being given the opportunity to preach to over 10,000 people by Dr. David A Newberry in a huge tent that was pitched opposite Chibuku Stadium in Chitungwiza.

An Assemblies of God (General Council) church was strengthened when a number of new converts joined that church as a result of that gospel campaign.

Dr. David A Newberry gave me other opportunities to preach at open air crusades that he conducted at Zororo Centre in Highfields, Harare. In the process I learned a lot of lessons in mass evangelism.

On the 8th and the 9th of April 2017, Dr. David A Newberry conducted two Miracle Services at our local church. It was a great privilege to host this great general and spiritual father in the faith.

The meetings were characterised by demonstrations of the power of God. There were a good number of instant healings, words of knowledge, words of wisdom and prophetic utterances.

My wife was healed during the course of these meetings from serious abdominal pains. She was supposed to go for more tests but when she was healed that was it. She did not need to go for more tests.

During these Miracle Services, Dr. David A Newberry spoke prophetic words over my life with the laying on of hands and prayers. This happened respectively on both days. On both occasions I fell down under the power of God as Dr. David A Newberry ministered to me.

I deeply treasure these encounters because I firmly believe that through these encounters there has been a transference of the anointings that operate in Dr. David A Newberry into my life.

A few years ago the Christian Union at the University of Zimbabwe invited me to minister the Word of God but unfortunately I could not make it due to some pressing ministry commitments.

I recommended Pastor Memory Mwangoh to Minister God's Word in my stead. However, the University of Zimbabwe Christian Union representative said that they were prepared to alter their dates to suite me.

I explained that Pastor Memory Mwangoh was a good minister of the Word of God and that if they accepted her they would be greatly blessed.

This was because I was aware that she flowed in the same anointing that I flowed in because she had received impartation of the anointing through the many meetings where

I had prayed for her by the laying on of hands and at times with dramatic encounters of God's power.

The University Christian Union representative eventually accepted that Pastor Mwangoh come and minister the Word of God in my place. And when Pastor Mwangoh ministered the Word of God at that meeting, the Lord used her mightily.

There was a mighty visitation of the Holy Spirit. There was holy pandemonium as many of the students were slain under the power of the Holy Ghost as she prayed for people with the laying on of hands.

Her husband who attended the meeting at the University of Zimbabwe, when he was giving me feedback of the meeting said, *"I was surprised to hear my wife tell people that she was going to count one up to four, and that at the count of four, the power of God was going to come down upon them and for sure the power of God did come upon them in a mighty way!"*

Impartation is serious business and really works. Be hungry and thirsty to be used by the Lord and place a demand on the anointing that you receive through impartation.

I am delighted to see people like Pastor Mwangoh and a host of other upcoming ministers flowing in the anointing with signs and wonders following as this makes me hopeful about the future.

We have a whole new generation of young ministers who are taking the relay button of the gospel further than we can ever do and it is a great joy for me to see that.

One of the values of impartation is continuity. God's program of reaching the lost must continue through upcoming generations of ministers.

During the 2016 Miracle Healing and Deliverance Services, I assigned Pastor Watson Chitate and Pastor Memory Mwangoh to preach the Word of God.

This was an unprecedented step that I felt led by the Lord to take. This was the first time since we started these services that I decided I would sit and not preach at all.

Pastor Chitate tried to convince me to choose another person but I firmly insisted that he would take to the pulpit. He eventually prepared to preach when he realized I was not joking.

When Pastor Chitate ministered, he powerfully preached the Word of God and took many people by surprise.

One of our Pastors even whispered to a congregant and said: *"Is this the Pastor Chitate we know?"* because of the way he powerfully ministered the Word of God and flowed in the anointing.

Pastor Mwangoh equally did justice once again by powerfully releasing the anointing as she ministered the Word of God in this gospel campaign dubbed Miracle Healing and Deliverance Services.

She later recounted during the campaign how she had on several occasions responded to alter calls for impartation of the anointing in similar meetings that I had conducted for a number of years.

Literally, all who have worked with me can flow in the anointings that operate in my life. Impartation is real and it works. One just needs to put a demand on the anointing that they would have received to see its manifestation.

4. Other Avenues Of Impartation

Impartation can come through many other mediums of communication like books, magazines, audio and video cassettes, films, the internet, music etc.

We must be very careful what we allow through these avenues of communication. If we don't regulate what we allow through these media platforms, we might end up sacrificing a whole new generation to the influence of the devil.

These media platforms are neither good nor evil in themselves. But the kind of stuff that is allowed to come through them determines that.

A lot of people who get hooked to pornography or violence and other perversions get hooked through impartation of the wrong stuff that they are exposed to through various media platforms.

Watching horror films can easily open up someone to demonic influences and nightmares.

We must always take an inventory of what sort of programmes our children are watching on the internet or television and where necessary parental control should be applied.

Soon after I was born again, I was exposed to Dr. T.L. Osborn's books and among these books were *The Three keys To the Book of Acts, The Purpose Of Pentecost, Soul Winning and Join This Chariot.*

Through these books the Lord ignited the passion in me to serve God. I could literally feel the burning fire of the Holy Ghost within me as I read those books.

I also used to receive Dr. T. L. Osborn's Faith Digest Magazine which contained colourful pictures of their evangelistic campaigns.

There were many testimonies of healing in those magazines. Some of the testimonies included the blind seeing, the lame walking and many other miracles of healing. In one of their Accra, Ghana campaigns, a child was raised from the dead.

It's this kind of material that made me hunger more and more for the miraculous dimension in my life and ministry. I developed a deep desire to help people find solutions to their perplexing problems through the anointing of God. It is one of the reasons I love the miraculous dimension of the anointing!

CONCLUSION

Impart what you are receivingthrough this book to others in the sphere of your influence. The more you give out, the more the Lord will give back into your life. Let others be partakers of your grace or anointing!

Philippians 1:7; 4:9(KJV)

*1.7...Ye **all** are partakers of **my grace.***

*4:9.Those things, which ye have **both learned**, and **received**, and **heard**, and **seen in me**, do: and the God of peace shall be with you.*

Allow yourself to be a conduit of impartation of the anointing to other people.Let there be beneficiation of the grace that is upon your life on other people.

Peter and John allowed themselves to be conduits of impartation when they *laid their hands on them (The new believers at Samaria), and they received the Holy Ghost.(Acts 8:17)KJV*

When the anointing is imparted to you, receive it by faith and learn to put a demand on it in order to experience its manifestation in your life

Chapter Four

DYNAMICS OF IMPARTATION

1. Impartation Can Come Through Association With Other Men or Women Of God

Mark 3:14-15(KJV)

*14. And He ordained twelve, that **they should be <u>with Him</u>**, and that he might **send them forth to preach**,*

*15.And **to have power to heal sicknesses, and to cast out devils:***

Jesus called His disciples *first of all **<u>to be with Him.</u>***

Since Jesus Christ was a good man His disciples were not corrupted by their association with Him. Instead the good that was upon Christ was imparted into their lives.

*Do not be misled: "**Bad company corrupts** good character" 1 Corinthians 15:33(New International Version)*

Jesus Christ was a good man *Who did not sin, neither was guile found in His mouth. (1 Peter 2:22)KJV*

Since the anointing can be imparted through association the anointing that was upon the Lord Jesus Christ was imparted upon His disciples as they spent time with Him.

Christ is the anointed one and His anointing will rub on you as you adide in Him. The rulers, elders and scribes *took knowledge of them (the disciples) that they **had been with Jesus** (Acts 4:13)KJV* because of the manifestation of the miraculous works of Christ in their lives and ministries.

2. Impartation Can Come Through The The Envirement That You Are Exposed To

The Disciples of Christ were exposed to a miraculous environment through the miraculous ministry of Christ.

You cannot be exposed to a miraculous environment without having something miraculous rubbing on you! In other words *the environment you are exposed to imparts something in you!*

One of the things that made me hunger for the supernatural was the manifestation of God's power that I witnessed in Bishop Stephen Mwale's life and ministry. That anointing was imparted into my life as I associated with Bishop Stephen Mwale in my early days of being a believer. I lived close to his house and I would visit once in a while and he would share some things about the ministry with me.

He once recounted how he had started out without furniture in his house but in due season the Lord blessed him with furniture. Through these interactions with him I received an impartation that enabled me to survive some of the rough patches of the ministry.

3. Impartation Can Come Through Anointed Influence

The Disciples of Christ came under the anointed influence of Christ through His teachings and manner of life.

*Whatever influence you come under will inevitably impart something in you.*The disciples received the impartation of the anointing that was upon the Lord Jesus Christ through His anointed influence.

Now when they saw the boldness of Peter and John, and perceived that they were unlearned and ignorant men, they marvelled; and they took knowledge of them, that they had been with Jesus.(Acts 4:13)KJV

Never underestimate the power of influence because a lot of impartation is received through influence.

4. Ministering To Other People Can Reveal The Anointing That One Has Received

After being **with** Christ for a while He was to *send them forth to preach, And to have power to heal sicknesses, and to cast out devils.(Mark 3:14, 15)KJV*

Mark 6:12, 13(KJV)

12. And they went out, and preached that men should repent.

13. And they cast out many devils, and anointed with oil many that were sick, and healed them.

After being with the Lord Jesus Christ for a while, the disciples were given opportunities to minister. And when they ministered, they flowed in the same anointing that the Lord Jesus flowed in. This fact showed that impartation of the anointing had indeed taken place.

After the resurrection of the Lord Jesus Christ, the disciples moved in a greater anointing.

*And with **great power** gave the apostles witness of the resurrection of the Lord Jesus: and **great grace** was upon them **all**.(Acts 4:33)KJV*

Not only did the impartation of a greater anointing come upon the disciples, it spilled over to the rest of the disciples (it came upon them **all**). *Impartation should permeate the whole church or organisation and not just a few members!*

I have given opportunities to minister to a lot of people in the course of my ministerial work as a way of releasing what was in them.

A good number of them are now ministers of the gospel. Had I not given them opportunities to minister, most of them would not have discovered the anointing that was upon them.

When God anoints you, He will provide opportunities for you to release the anointing that He has placed upon you. You don't have to fight for that especially when it seems like you have been overlooked or ignored by those in authority. In His time God makes all things beautiful.

At one time as I served as an assistant pastor I was given ample opportunities to be a master of ceremonies but not to preach by the senior pastor. However, one of the elders was given many chances to preach by the senior pastor.

Some members of the congregation brought this to my attention but I graciously told them that I was there to serve in whatever capacity my senior pastor assigned me. Honestly I had no hard feelings over this and I did not wrongly judge the senior pastor in anyway.

If one is not careful, its easy to split the church over issues of this nature. But we must beware of the schemes of the enemy who always seek to take advantage of any situation. We must not allow pride to cloud our judgement.

Then time came when another senior pastor gave me a lot of chances to preach so much that the wife of the other co-pastor bitterly complained about this seemingly favoritism.

Learn to trust God to give you opportunities to release the anointing that He has placed upon you.

Don't get agitated if you seem to be overlooked while others seem to be given more opportunities to minister. If the Lord has truly anointed you, He will make a way for you in His own way and in His own time! Do not let such scenariors cause you to clandestinely begin to campaign for opportunities to minister.

Sometimes we may think we are the greatest thing that ever happened in our organisation when in reality that is not the case.

Sometimes God maybe humbling us when we are not thrust in the limelight that we so much desire to be in!

Be clothed with humility:for God resisteth the proud, and giveth grace to the humble. Humble yourselves therefore under the mighty hand of God, that He may exalt you in due time(1Peter 5:5,6)KJV

5. Impartation Can Come Through Ministering To Our Leaders

*And he returnèd back from him, and took a yoke of oxen, and slew them, and boiled their flesh with the instruments of the oxen, and gave unto the people, and they did eat. Then he arose, and went after Elijah, and **ministered unto him**.(1 Kings 19:21)KJV* Elisha became

Elijah's servant. He served him by pouring water on the hands of Elijah and doing many other odd tasks for Elijah.

There is a powerful impartation that one is able to access through servanthood. Many great men and women of God served other servants of the Lord and in the process ended up tapping into the anointings of those that they served.

But Jehoshaphat said, Is there not here a prophet of the Lord that we may enquire of the Lord by him? And one of the king of Israel's servants answered and said, Here is Elisha the son of Shaphat, **which poured water on the hands of Elijah.***(2 Kings 3:11)KJV* When Jehosphat inquired for a good prophet, the one that came to mind was Elisha who had served Elijah.

Elisha in serving Elijah ended up receiving a double portion of the anointing that was upon Elijah. (2Kings 2:9-14)KJV

And Joshua the son of Nun was full of the spirit of wisdom; For **Moses had laid his hands upon him***: and the children of Israel hearkened unto him, and did as the LORD commanded Moses. (Deuteronomy 34:9)KJV*

Joshua received the impartation of the spirit of wisdom through the ministration of the laying on of hands by Moses. Faithfully serving Moses positioned him rightly to receive that impartation.

Now after the death of Moses the servant of the LORD it came to pass, that the LORD spake unto Joshua the son of Nun, **Moses' minister,***saying...(Joshua1:1)KJV*

Joshua was Moses' minister or servant. Serving other men and women of God is a great avenue to receiving mighty impartations of the anointing from the men and women of God in your life.

Never take such opportunities for granted because such opportunities can result in you tapping into the anointing of your leader.

6. Impartation And Leadership Change

And the LORD spake unto Moses face to face as a man speaketh unto his friend. And he turned again into the camp: **but His servant Joshua the son of Num, a young man, departed not out of the tabernacle.***(Exodus 33:11)KJV* Joshua served Moses so well that he departed not out of the tabernacle. He did this in order to effectively serve Moses.

Joshua positioned himself in the best position for serving Moses. He did not do this with the motive of eventually taking over from Moses but rather to minister to Moses so that

Moses can successfully fulfil his God given role. Have that attitude. That is the attitude of true servanthood.

Numbers 27:16-20(KJV)

*16. **Let the LORD**, the God of the spirits of all flesh, **set a man over the congregation**,*

17. Which may go out before them, and which may lead them out, and which may bring them in; that the congregation of the LORD be not as sheep which have no shepherd.

*18. **And the LORD said unto Moses, Take thee Joshua the son of Nun, a man in whom is the Spirit, and lay thine hand upon him;***

19. And set him before Eleazar the priest, and before all the congregation; and give him a charge in their sight.

20. And thou shalt put some of thine honour upon him, that all the congregation of the Children of Israel maybe obedient.

It was the Lord Himself that chose Joshua when Moses inquired about this issue from thre Lord. Joshua did not choose himself and neither did Moses choose Joshua.

Moses knew that he was about to leave and a leadership transition was imminent. He wisely inquired of the Lord.

Leaders however, have a responsibility to mentor other leaders so that there is continuity. *Success without a successor is really no success at all. Good and smooth leadership transitions are not usualy accidental.*

Some leaders may retire or change from functioning in certain tasks to other roles within or outside the organisation. It is important to know how to treat such leaders by affording them the honour and respect and support due to them. Have the wisdom to maintain a healthy relationship with such people and draw from their experience and wisdom.

Issues of succession work smoothly when mentors do their part by mentoring their protégés and ensuring that an enabling environment for smooth transition is in place. This is so that when the need arises for leadership change it is done smoothly without throwing an organisation and people into a crisis.

It is wise for key leaders to have several protégés. Succession should be well executed through conscious mentorship and passing on of essential values and good timing.

It is important that we all realise that sometimes a new leader may have a different personality, anointing and emphasis.

There is however one constant in life that we must all come to terms with. And that constant is *change*!

It is not easy to deal with change and yet change is a fact of life that we all have to deal with.

7. Impartation And Future Generations

And it came to pass after these things, that Joshua the son of Num, the servant of the LORD, died, being a hundred and ten years old. **And Israel served the LORD all the days of Joshua, and all the days of the elders that outlived Joshua,** *and which had known all the works of the LORD that He had done for Israel.(Joshua 24:29)KJV*

Judges 2:10-15(KJV)

10. And also all the generation were gathered unto their fathers: and **there arose another generation after them, which knew not the LORD, nor yet the works which he had done for Israel.**

11. **And the children of Israel did evil in the sight of the LORD, and served Baalim:**

12. And they forsook the LORD God of their fathers, which brought them out of Egypt, and followed other gods, of the gods of the people that were round about them, and bowed themselves unto them, and provoked the LORD to anger.

13. And they forsook the LORD, and served Baal and Ashtaroth.

14. **And the anger of the LORD was hot against Israel, and he delivered them into the hands of spoilers that spoiled them, and He sold them into the hands of their enemies round about, so that they could no longer stand before their enemies.**

15.Withersoever they went out, the hand of the LORD was against them for evil, as the LORD had said, and as the LORD had sworn unto them: and they were greatly distressed.

It seems that when the elders that outlived Joshua passed on, a disconnection occurred because there arose a new generation that did not know the Lord. And that generation did a lot of evil.

It is not easy to capture generations for the Lord but that's what we have to work at.We have to impart the knowledge of the Lord from one generation to the other lest we end up with generations that do not know the Lord.

Nevertheless the LORD raised up judges, which delivered them out of the hand of those that spoiled them.(Judges 2:16)KJV

Moses raised up Joshua. Joshua raised up the elders who eventually outlived him. But who did the elders raise? Could this be responsible for the disconnection that eventually brought up a generation that knew not the Lord? Elders have the responsibility of positively affecting upcoming generations.

*Do not neglect the gift which is in you, [that special inward endowment] which was directly imparted to you [by the Holy Spirit] by prophetic utterance **when the elders laid their hands upon you [at your ordination]**.1 Timothy 4:14 Amplified Bible Classic Edition(AMPC)*

Elders played a very significant role in the life of Timothy who was a young and upcoming minister of the gospel. **Elders should function in their roles lest we end up with a disconnection in upcoming generations!**

Some leaders may not necessarily be called elders but in function they are elders. Elders usually have an oversight resposnsibility. It is critically important for elders to take their responsibilities seriously because many generations depend on their critical role.

8. Impartation Of Lifestyle

2 Timothy 3:10, 14(KJV)

*10. But thou hast fully known my doctrine,**manner of life**, purpose, faith, longsuffering, charity,patience,*

*14.But **continue** thou in the things which thou **hast learned** and **hast been assured of**, **knowing of whom thou hast learned them**.*

While it is a good thing to receive an impartation of the anointing resting upon someone, it is much more important to receive the manner of life of that person, especially if it is godly.

The lifestyle or the manner of life that a mentor exposes a protégé to and what a protégé emulates from his or her mentor will largely determine how far that protégé will go.

While following mentors is a natural outcome of protégés, protégés must avoid any unbiblical practices that a mentor may engage in. A lot of care and respect must be exercised when avoiding the mistakes of a mentor. Don't throw the baby with the bathwater as this common adage says. Have the wisdom to keep the good that you need to keep and avoid the bad that you need to avoid.

I am saying this because mentors are not perfect and may make mistakes. *It is critically important for protégés to be able to do the right thing in the face of a mentor's mistakes and yet still have a healthy respect for the mentor.*

There are some protégés who have ended up following in the mistakes of their mentors and in the end they have negatively affected their lives.

This is why it is important for mentors to set good examples for their protégés. *Neither as being lords over God's heritage, but being ensamples to the flock.(1 Peter 5:3)KJV*

Mentors on the other hand should lovingly correct their protégés if they make mistakes. That's how we raise good men and women of God who will carry the relay button stick of the gospel further than we can ever carry it.

9. Impartation Through Believers' Homes

Proper impartation of godly values must be passed on from generation to generation through parental influence.

Our own homes should be the most powerful places where our children receive the impartation of the anointing. Our children must be so impacted by our very lives that in turn they positively impact the lives of their children and the cycle continues through great grandchildren's upcoming generations!

That is how we can culture or nurture generations long after we are gone.

Deuteronomy 6:2-18(KJV)

*2. **That thou mightiest fear the LORD thy God, to keep all His statutes and His commandments, which I command thee, thou, and thy son, and thy son's son, all the days of thy life; and that thy days may be prolonged.***

3. **Hear therefore, O Israel, and observe to do it; that it may be well with thee; and that ye may increase mightily,** *as the LORD God of thy fathers hath promised thee, in the land that floweth with milk and honey.*

4. *Hear, O Israel: The LORD our God is one LORD:And thou shalt love the LORD thy God with all thine heart, and with all thy soul, and with all thy might.*

6. **And these words, which I command thee this day,shall be in thine heart:**

7. *And thou shalt* **teach them diligently unto thy children,** *and* **shalt talk of them** *when thou* **sittest in thine house,** *and when thou* **walkest by the way,** *and when thou* **liest down,** *and when thou* **risest up.**

8.*And thou shalt* **bind them** *for a sign upon* **thine hand,** *and they shall be as frontlets between* **thine eyes.**

9. *And thou shalt* **write** *them* **upon** *the* **posts of thy house,** *and* **on thy gates.**

10. *And it shall be, when the LORD thy God shall have brought thee into the land which He sware unto thy fathers, to Abraham, to Isaac, and to Jacob, to give thee great and goodly cities, which thou buildedst not,*

11.*And* **houses full of all good things,** *which thou* **filledst not,** *and wells digged, which thou* **diggedst not,** *vineyards and olive trees, which thou* **plantedst not;** *when thou shalt have eaten and be full;*

12. *Then beware lest thou forget the LORD, which brought thee forth out of the land of Egypt, from the house of bondage.*

13. *Thou shalt fear the LORD thy God, and serve him, and shalt swear by His name.*

14.*Ye shall not go after other gods, of the gods of the people which are round about you;*

15. **(For the LORD thy God is a jealous God among you) lest the anger of the LORD thy God be kindled against thee, and destroy thee from off the face of the earth.**

16. *Thou shall not tempt the LORD your God, as ye tempted Him in Massah.*

17. Ye shall diligently keep the commandments of the LORD your God, and His testimonies, and His statutes, which He hath commanded thee.

*18. And **thou shalt do that which is right and good in the sight of the LORD: that it may be well with thee, and that thou mayest go in and possess the good land which the LORD sware unto thy fathers.***

Parents due to their position in the lives of their children are in the most powerful position of all human relationships to impart the anointing to their children.

The Lord knows the influence that parents wield over their children. And parents ought to know that and take responsibility to impart that to their children.

10. Impartation And The Release Of Needed Human Resources

Ephesians 4:11, 12(KJV)

11. And He gave some, apostles; and some, prophets; and some, evangelists; and some, pastors and teachers;

12. for the perfecting of the saints, for the work of the ministry, for the edifying of the body of Christ:

The reason why the Lord gave the fivefold ministry gifts is for the perfecting or equipping of the saints or believers for the work of the ministry. When this is done properly it culminates in the edification and growth of the body of Christ, which is the church.

*The fivefold ministry gifts are specialist gifts so to speak! They are there to train the saints for the work of the ministry so that the saints can **actually do the work of the ministry**!*

In fact, as far as the Lord's plan for the church is concerned, every believer is supposed to be a minister!

But the way we have sometimes structured our churches in many situations tends to turn saints into spectators.

The church should be the most powerful training centre because of the impartation factor.

Saints are supposed to tap into the anointing of the ministry gifts for the purpose of doing the work of the ministry.

Ephesians 4:13-16(KJV)

13. Till we all come in the unity of the faith, and of the knowledge of the Son of God,unto a perfect man, unto the measure of the stature of the fullness of Christ:

*14.**That we henceforth be no more children, tossed to and fro, and carried about with every wind of doctrine, by the sleight of men, and cunning craftiness, whereby they lie in wait to deceive;***

15. But speaking the truth in love, may grow up into Him in all things, which is the head, even Christ:

*16.**From** whom **the whole body fitly joined together** and **compacted** by that which **every joint supplieth,** according to **the effectual working in the measure of every part,** maketh increase of the body unto the edifying of itself in love.*

When Moses had the challenge of being overwhelmed by the burden of the work of shepherding the Children of Israel he cried out to the Lord and said *"I am not able to bear all this people alone, because it is too heavy for me"(Numbers 11:14)*

Numbers 11:16-17(KJV)

*16. And the LORD said unto Moses, Gather unto me seventy men of the elders of Israel whom thou knowest to be the elders of the people, and officers of the people, and officers over them; and bring them unto the tabernacle of the congregation, **that they may stand with thee.***

*17. And I will come down and talk with thee: **and I will take of the spirit which is upon thee, and I will put it upon them; and they shall bear the burden of the people with thee, that thou bear it not thyself alone.***

The Lord Himself administered the impartation by taking the Spirit that was upon Moses and imparting it upon the leaders so that they could bear the burden of the people with Moses and thus lightening the burden for Moses.

It's important that those working with the set man or woman of God have the same spirit and a God given burden to carry out their functions of assisting the set man or set woman of God.

Through impartation every saint should be turned into a minister, and in the process an abundance of able ministers should be mobilised for the advancement of the kingdom of God.

CONCLUSION

Peter knew he had the healing anointing. That is why he was able to confidently say ...***Such as I have give I thee****: In the name of Jesus Christ of Nazareth rise up and walk. (Acts 3:6)KJV*

Every saint must know the anointing that rests upon him or her and release that anointing so that people are ministered to wherever the saints come in contact with people that need the touch of God.

Dear reader know what you are anointed to do and do it!

You have to know that you have the anointing for you to confidently release it for the benefit of other people

Chapter Five

MUSIC AND THE ANOINTING

There are many music genres. Among these are traditional gospel, contemporary gospel, country music, rock 'n' roll, soul music, jazz, rhumba etc. For a comprehensive list of music genres check this website: www.musicgenreslist.com

Each genre carries with it a certain inspiration and has the power to capture the hearts of its listeners.

In 1997, I attended Celebration Church's Action '97 Conference that was held at the Harare International Conference Centre. Celebration Church was then known as Hear The Word Ministries.

1. The Power Of Godly Spiritual Music

I witnessed Kent Henry singing and playing the piano at this conference. As he sang the power of God literally invaded that auditorium in a mighty way. Healings and deliverances took place as many people fell under the power of God. There was no laying on of hands and there was such a deep sense of God's Presence and power!

Spiritual music is an avenue through which the anointing can be received and released. *The right song at the right time can usher in a powerful anointing.*

Equally true as well is the fact that the wrong song at the wrong time can stop or quench the flow of the anointing.

It is therefore important for those leading music teams to be very sensitive to the Spirit. At times the minister may not mention the song that the music leader must sing but trust that the music leader will pick the right song by the unction of the Holy Spirit.

In 2009, I attended the *Joseph Anointing Miracle Service* conducted by Apostle P W Mbewe of Calvary Church, Malawi. The meeting took place at the Harare Polytechnic College Hall. The preaching of the Word of God was highly anointed and mighty demonstrations of God's power were displayed when Apostle Mbewe started praying for people.

One thing that clearly stood out in this powerful meeting was the way music played a big role in activating and releasing the anointing.

Once the man of God had finished preaching, the music team started singing the song *"There is one thing I know, everywhere I go, that Jesus' love has never failed me yet..."* The power of God would start moving amongst the people, with many people falling under the power of God without anybody touching them.

Many people experienced healing and deliverance during ministration.

*But now bring me a minstrel. And it came to pass, when the minstrel played, **that the hand of the LORD came upon him**.(2 Kings 3:15)KJV*

It was only when the minstrel had played that the hand of the Lord came upon Elisha and then he prophesied. *The hand of the Lord speaks of the anointing.* It was the music that activated the anointing.

Several armies that consisted the children of Moab, the children of Ammon and Mount Seir came against King Jehoshaphat. The armies were too numerous for him to contend with.

King Jehoshaphat was naturally afraid and proclaimed a fast throughout all Judah to seek the Lord and the help of the Lord. *(2Chronicles 20:1-30)KJV*

After some prophetic words were given to encourage the people of Judah, a simple strategy was employed by the children of Judah at the direction of the Lord.

2 Chronicles 20:21-24(KJV)

*21.And when he had consulted with the people, **he appointed singers unto the LORD**, and that **they should praise the beauty of holiness**, as they went out before the army, and to say, **Praise the LORD; for his mercy endureth for ever.***

*22.And **when they began to sing and to praise, the LORD set ambushments against the children of Ammon**, Moab, and mount Seir, which were come against Judah; and they were smitten,*

23. For the children of Ammon and Moab stood up against the inhabitants of mount Seir, utterly to slay and destroy them: and when they had made an end of the inhabitants of Seir, every one helped to destroy another.

*24. And when Judah came toward the watch tower in the wilderness, they looked unto the multitude, and, behold, they were dead bodies fallen to the earth, and **none escaped**.*

It was when they began to sing and to praise the Lord that the Lord set up ambushments and confusion in the camp of the enemy. That was a release of power in unprecedented dimensions. Never underestimate the power that can be released through music!

This was a real war and yet music proved to be the key to victory!

We have another example where the power of the Lord was released through music.

2Chronicles 5:13, 14(KJV)

*13. It came to pass, as **the trumpeters** and **singers** were **as one, to make one sound to be heard in praising and thanking the LORD**; and when they **lifted up their voice** with the **trumpets** and **cymbals** and **instruments of music**, and **praised the LORD, saying, For He is good; for His mercy endureth forever**: that then the **house was filled with a cloud**, even the house of the LORD;*

*14. So that the priests **could not stand to minister by reason of the cloud**: for the glory of the LORD filled the house of God.*

The glory of the Lord filled the house of the Lord in the form of a cloud. Sometimes the glory of the Lord is spoken of as the heaviness of His Presence.

The glory cloud was so heavy that the priests could not stand to minister! Simply put in easy to understand language they were laying down on the ground! They must have began by standing only to go down as the glory cloud filled the house!

Music releases the anointing of God in powerful ways that we have only scratched the tip of the iceberg in this matter!

In our Miracle Healing and Deliverance Services and other special services sufficient time is given for praise and worship and often the anointing of God is activated and released in a powerful way.

*And it came to pass, when the evil spirit from God was upon Saul, that David took an harp, and played with His hand: so Saul **was refreshed**, and **was well,** and the evil spirit departed from him.(1 Samuel 16:23)KJV*

David was a skilful player of the harp. Somehow the people in the days of Saul understood the power of music such that when David played the harp, the evil spirit would leave Saul and he would be refreshed.

Good spiritual music can bring spiritual refreshment,revival,renewal,healing and restoration.

In (James 5:13)KJV, the Word of God clearly states, *Is any among you afflicted? Let him pray. Is any merry?* ***Let him sing psalms.***

*And when they (Jesus Christ and His disciples) had **sang out a hymn**, they went out into the Mount of Olives.(Mark 14:26)KJV*

Ephesians 5:18-19(KJV)

18. And be not drunk withwine, wherein in excess; but be filled with the Spirit.

*19. **Speaking to yourselves** in **psalms** and **hymns** and **spiritual songs, singing** and **making melody in your hearts to the Lord.***

Godly spiritual music unleashes the power of God. Through good spiritual music people are inspired to godliness and good moral ethics.

2. The Power Of Evil Music

Through secular music, most of which is inspired by the devil, many people have been influenced for evil. Consumption of illicity drugs, illicit sex, devil worship, suicide, wicked suggestive dancing and excessive alcohol consumption are some of the by-products of evil music.

The deception of worldly music is so tricky that most of the people who are engaged in it do not even realise that they are being influenced by the devil through worldly music.

God has this to say about worldly music, *Take thou away from me the noise of thy songs; for I will not hear the melody of thy viols.(Amos 5:23)KJV*

Those anointed to minister in music must take this ministry seriously and adhere to its demands especially virtues like prayer, discipline, teamwork,dedication, humility and sensitivity to the Holy Spirit.

The devil tries hard to hinder those ministering in the area of music simply because it is one of the most powerful ways in which to receive and release the anointing.

The devil is subtle and tries to infiltrate church choirs and Christian music teams by sowing discord and confusion among them. *This is why it is important that Christian music teams pray together and overcome every scheme of the enemy.*

The devil understands the power of music because God's Word, when speaking of the devil says,*the workmanship of thy tabrets and thy pipes was prepared in thee in the day that thou was created. Thou art the* **anointed** *cherub that covereth; and I have set thee so: thou was upon the holy mountain of God; thou has walked up and down in the midst of the stones of fire. (Ezekiel 28:13-14)KJV*

According to the above scripture, the devil was actually at one time a musician who had music pipes within his very being and was the anointed cherub that was heavily involved in leading worship of the Almighty God in heaven.

Since the devil was a musician, one of the areas he uses to deceive many people is through worldly music. It is amazing how many people have been captured for the kingdom of darkness through this worldly music.

This is why it is so important for Christian musicians to rise and take their place in influencing our generations for the Lord lest we lose them to the devil!

CONCLUSION

The devil understands the real power of music and seeks to hinder spiritual music. But we must not give him any room at all. *Neither give place to the devil.(Ephesians 4:27)KJV* Instead we must ensure that good godly spiritual music is given its rightful place.

The devil tries very hard to hinder those ministering in the area of music simply because it's one of the most powerful ways in which the anointing is received and released

Chapter Six

HOW TO INCREASE THE ANOINTING THAT IS UPON YOU

The anointing that is upon your life can increase or decrease depending on how you handle it. Manage it well and it will increase. Manage it badly and it will decrease.

Here are some things that you can do in order to increase the anointing that is upon your life:

1. Loving Righteousness And Hating Iniquity

*Thou Hast loved righteousness, and hated iniquity; therefore God, even thy God, hath **anointed thee with the oil** of gladness <u>above</u> thy fellows.(Hebrews 1:9)KJV*

Let thy garments be always white (this symbolically speaks of righteousness); and let thy head lack no ointment (The anointing) (Ecclesiastes9:8)KJV

If you desire a greater anointing in your life, learn to love righteousness and to hate iniquity. Have a clear understanding that you are dealing with the "Holy Spirit" who is holy and righteous.

Therefore *impurity or ungodliness will cause the anointing to decrease in your life while purity and godliness will cause the anointing to increase in your life.*

1 Peter 1:14-16(KJV)

14.As obedient children, not fashioning yourselves according to the former lusts in your ignorance:

*15.But as He which hath called you **is holy**, so **be ye holy** in all manner of conversation; because it is written, **be ye holy; for I am holy.***

*Having therefore these promises, dearly beloved, **let us cleanse ourselves from all filthiness of the flesh and spirit, perfecting holiness in the fear of God.**(2 Corinthians 7:1)KJV*

It is those who love righteousness and hate iniquity that God anoints with the oil of gladness **above** their fellows.

Somehow unrighteousness short-circuits the anointing of God in our lives. Purity attracts and increases the anointing in our lives. Purpose to walk in purity.

2. Fervent Prayer

*The earnest (heartfelt, continued) prayer of a righteous man **makes tremendous power available, [dynamic in its working]**.(James 5:16(b) Amplified Bible Classic Edition (AMPC)*

The tremendous power that is being spoken of here is the anointing. Tremendous power speaks of ***greater power.*** If you desire an increase in the anointing that is upon your life, earnest prayer is the key. God's Word admonishes us to *Pray without ceasing in 1 Thessalonians 5:17(KJV)*

Luke 5:16, 17(KJV)

*16. And He (Jesus) withdrew himself into the wilderness, and **prayed**.*

17. And it came to pass on a certain day, as he was teaching, that there were Pharisees and the doctors of law sitting by, which were come out of every village of Galilee and Judaea and Jerusalem: **and the power of the Lord was present to heal them**.

The power of the Lord is the healing anointing which was made available through prayer. Neglecting prayer can decrease the anointing in your life.

3. Prayer And Fasting

Luke 4:1-2(KJV)

1. And Jesus being full of the Holy Ghost returned from Jordan, and was led by the Spirit into the wilderness,

2. Being forty days tempted of the devil. And in those days He did eat nothing: and when they were ended, He afterward hungered. Jesus fasted for 40 days and 40 nights. Although the word prayer is absent from these scriptures,Jesus prayed and fasted.

And Jesus returned in the **power of the Spirit** *into Galilee: and there went out a* **fame of Him through the entire region round about**.*(Luke 4:14)KJV*

At one time the disciples tried to cast a demon out a boy who was possessed by a demon. They failed to cast that demon out. However the Lord Jesus Christ cast that demon out without any struggle.

When the disciples inquired why they could not cast that demon out,the Lord Jesus Christ told them, *"This kind* **can come forth by nothing, but by prayer and fasting.***"(Mark 9:29)KJV*

There are situations in life that only prayer and fasting can deal with. Prayer and fasting increases the anointing upon your life.

Some people with health issues like sugar diabetes, high blood pressure, pregnancy and those on prescription drugs, etc. should consult their doctors for advice before proceeding with the fast.

I had a minister friend who had very strong convictions in this area of prayer and fasting. We however lost him when he suffered ulcers due to the extreme way he exercised this discipline.

Beware that any doctrine can be taken to extremes if we are not careful to rightly divide the Word of truth. There is need for exercising this discipline with wisdom and balance in order to reap good results as intended by the Lord.

Fasting should be done with right motives. It must not be used as a bargaining chip designed to twist the hand of God.

When you fast, you are surrendering to the will and purpose of God. Fasting increases the anointing which makes it easy to break yokes or bondages.

*Is not this **the fast that I have chosen**? **To loose the bands of wickedness, to undo the heavy burdens, and to let the oppressed go free, and that ye break every yoke?***(Isaiah 58:6)KJV*

I cannot carry out some of the special meetings like the Miracle Healing and Deliverance Services, Night of Miracles, Super Sunday or Holy Ghost Power Services without investing time in prayer and fasting.

This is because we expect the power and anointing of God to move in a special way in such meetings. The manifestation of God's power in these services is often at a greater level due to the spiritual investment through prayer and fasting.

If you genuinely desire to receive a greater anointing in your life, then from time to time invest your time in prayer and fasting.

Neglecting prayer and fasting decreases the anointing. Since your desire is to have a greater anointing in your life, take care that you do not neglect the discipline of prayer and fasting.

4. Praying In The Holy Ghost

*But ye, beloved, building yourselves on your most holy faith, **praying in the Holy Ghost.** (Jude 1:20)KJV*

Praying in the Holy Ghost is praying in other tongues. For if I pray in unknown tongue, my spirit prayeth, but my understanding is unfruitful. (1Corinthians 14:14)KJV Although my mind does not understand what I am saying when I pray in the Holy Ghost, I am personally strengthened.

For he that speaketh in unknown tongue edifieth (strengthens) himself. (1Corithians 14:14)KJV

The idea behind this is that of recharging oneself spiritually. In the same way that we recharge our cellphone batteries one recharges himself or herself spiritually by speaking in other tongues.

This is why Paul in *1Corinthians 14:18(KJV)* says, *I thank my God, I speak with tongues more than ye all.* Paul apparently spent considerable amounts of time praying in the Spirit. This activity stirs and increases the anointing in one's life.

There are more than 7 dimensions to speaking in other tongues. One of those dimensions is the one I am talking about. So spend considerable amounts of time praying in the Holy Ghost.

*Wherefore I put thee in remembrance that thou **stir up** the gift of God, which is thee by the laying of my hands.(2Timothy 1:6)KJV* Praying in other tongues stirs the anointing.

5. Flowing In Unity

Psalm 1:1-3(KJV)

1. Behold, how good and how pleasant for brethren to dwell together in unity!

2. It is like precious ointment upon the head that ran down upon the beard even Aaron's bead: that went down to the skirts of his garments;

*3.As the dew of Hermon, and as the dew that descended upon the mountains of Zion: for there the LORD commanded **the blessing**, even life for evermore.*

Unity brings an increase in the anointing and lack of unity decreases the anointing in a corporate body of believers.

They **were all with one accord in one place***(Acts 2:1)*KJV when the Holy Ghost descended upon the disciples on the day of Pentecost. They were united. They continued *"With one accord"(Acts 2:46)KJV*

No wonder there was such a great anointing that was released upon them! *And with great power gave the apostles witness of the Lord Jesus: and great grace was upon them all. (Acts 4:33)KJV*

6. Being Clothed With Humility

God's Word admonishes us **to be clothed with humility:** *for God resisteth the proud, and **giveth grace to the humble.**(1Peter 5:5)KJV*

But **He giveth more grace.** *Wherefore He saith, God resisteh the proud, but giveth grace unto the humble. (James 4:6)KJV* More grace speaks of a greater measure of the anointing.

Do not be pompous. Be clothed with the garment of humility.How do you do that? Well, God's Word gives us some ideas through these verses: *Don't be selfish; don't try to impress others.* **Be humble, thinking of others as being better than yourselves.** *Philippians 2:3(New Living Tlanslation)*

For through the authority graciously given to me I warn every individual among you **not to value himself unduly**, *but* **to cultivate sobriety of judgement** *in accordance with the amount of faith which God Has allotted to each one. Romans 12:3 Weymouth New Testament(WNT)*

Humility attracts and increases the anointing. This is because humility is an attitude of dependence upon the Lord. May we receive the grace to walk in humility.

Humble yourselves in the sight of the Lord, and He shall lift you up. (James 4:10)KJV

Humble yourselves therefore under the mighty hand of God, that He may exalt you in due time: (I Peter 5:6)KJV

Therefore, as God's chosen people, holy and dearly loved, **clothe yourselves** *with* **compassion, kindness, humility, gentleness** *and* **patience**. *Colossians 3:2(New International Version)*

Finally, all of you, be likeminded, be sympathetic,*love one another, be compassionate and* **humble.** *1 Peter 3:8(New International Version)*

Pride causes the anointing to decrease in your life. Somehow God withdraws His grace from the proud and even goes further by resisting the proud! Pride is a wicked virtue that you must simply not entertain in your life!

7. Be Faithful In Managing The Anointing That Is Upon You.

He that is **faithful in that which is least** *is* **faithful also in much**: *and he that is* **unjust in the least is unjust also in much**. *(Luke 16:10)KJV*

Faithfulness in managing the anointing that we receive from the Lord positions us for increase in the anointing. Conversely, unfaithfulness in managing the anointing that we receive from the Lord will inevitably result in the decrease of the anointing.

Paul was faithful in managing the anointing that was placed upon his life and consequently experienced increase in the anointing that was upon his life. It took years of faithful service and shifts in his scopes of operation to get to the apostolic phase!

Most men will proclaim everyone his own goodness: **but a faithful man who can find?***(Proverbs 20:6)KJV* Faithfully manage the anointing that the Lord has placed upon your life because that is what brings increase in the level of the anointing that is upon your life.

*As every man hath received the gift, even so minister the same one to another, **as good stewards of the manifold grace of God**.(1Peter 4:10)KJV* Be a good steward or manager of the anointing that is upon your life.

***Neglect not the gift that is in thee**, which was given thee by prophesy, with the laying on of the hands of the presbytery.(1 Timothy 4:14)KJV*

Paul did not begin his ministry as an apostle but as a simple but powerful preacher of the Good News of Jesus Christ soon after his conversion.

Acts9:20, 28, 29(KJV)

20.And straightway he preached Christ in the synagogues, that he is the Son of God.

28. And he was with them coming in and going out of Jerusalem.

29. And he spake boldly in the name of the Lord Jesus, and disputed against the Grecians: but they went about to slay him

But Saul (This is of course speaking of Paul) ***increased the more in strength**, and confounded the Jews which dwelt at Damascus, proving that this is the Christ.(Acts9:22)KJV*
In *Acts 13:1(KJV) Paul is said to be among the **prophets** and **teachers** that were at Antioch together with Barnabas.*

Paul graduated from being just a preacher of the gospel to being a prophet and a teacher.

Acts 13:2-4(KJV)

*2. As they ministered to the Lord, and fasted, the Holy Ghost said, **Separate me Barnabas and Saul for the work where unto I have called them**.*

3. And when they had fasted and prayed, and laid their hands on them, they sent them away.

4. So they, being sent forth by the Holy Ghost, departed unto Seleucia; and from thence they sailed to Cyprus

Here Barnabas and Saul were ushered into another phase of their ministries by the Lord. Barnabas and Paul's ministries entered the apostolic phase after this encounter. For shortly after this encounter Barnabas and Paul were for the first time called apostles. *...When **the apostles Barnabas and Paul**... (Acts 14:14)KJV*

Paul experienced progression and increase in the anointing that was upon his life as he faithfully served the Lord.

CONCLUSION

*Be not deceived; God is not mocked: **for whatsoever a man soweth, that shall he also reap.**(Galatians 6:7)KJV*

Extraordinary preparation brings extraordinary results. Remember that when you pray and fast you are spiritually sowing or investing in an extra-ordinary way.

Learn to steward the anointing that the Lord Has placed upon your life in a way that causes it to increase rather than to decrease

Chapter Seven

HOW TO RELEASE THE ANOINTING THAT IS UPON YOU

It is a good thing to receive the anointing and increase that anointing. However, it is equally of great importance to be able to effectively release that anointing for the benefit and good of other people.

Here are some of the ways in which you can release the anointing that is upon you:

1. Ministering The Word of God

One of the most powerful avenues of releasing the anointing is the preaching of the gospel of Christ.

Mark 16:15, 17-18, 20(KJV)

15. And he said unto them, Go ye into all the world, and preach the gospel to every creature.

17. And these signs shall follow them thatbelieve; In my name shall they cast out devils; they shall speak with new tongues;

18. They shall take up serpents; and if they drink any deadly thing, it shall not hurt them; they shall lay hands on the sick, and they shall recover.

20. And they went forth, and preached everywhere, **the Lord working with them,** *and* **confirming the Word with signs following.** *Amen. Please take note the Lord confirms the* **Word.** *Therefore proclaim the* **Word!** *God has nothing to confirm if the* **Word** *is not proclaimed.*

Through preaching the gospel, the anointing is released. *For I am not ashamed of the gospel of Christ: for it is the* **power** *of God unto salvation... (Romans 1:16)KJV*

Unto whom it was revealed, that not unto themselves, but unto you, did they minister the things, which are now reported unto you by them that have **preached the gospel unto you with the Holy Ghost sent down from heaven;** *which things angels desire to look into. (1 Peter 1:12)KJV*

2. Flowing In Your Anointing

Peter spoke of *How God anointed Jesus of Nazareth with the Holy Ghost and with power:***Who went about doing good,** *and* **healing all that were oppressed of the devil;** *for God was with Him. (Acts 10:38)KJV* Jesus simply flowed in the anointing that was upon Him.

The anointing does not come upon you for decoration. It comes upon you so that you can flow in that anointing for the benefit of other people.

If any man speak, let him speak as the oracles of God; **if any man minister,** *let him do it as of the* **ability***(or the anointing) which God giveth: that God in all things may be glorified through Jesus Christ, to whom be praise and dominion for ever and ever. Amen. (1 Peter 4:11)KJV*

What this verse is telling us is that if the anointing that is upon you is to preach God's Word, then flow effectively in that preaching anointing! Learn to flow in whatever anointing the Lord has placed upon your life.

Christ spoke that He that believeth on Him, *as the scripture hath said, out of his belly(or innermost being) shall **flow rivers of living water**. (John 7:38)KJV*

(But this spake He of the Spirit (or the anointing) which they that believe on Him should receive: for the Holy Ghost was not yet given; because that Jesus was not yet glorified) John 7:39 (KJV)

*I believe that the river spoken of in Ezekiel 47:7 (KJV)speaks metaphorically of the Holy Spirit. Swarms of living creatures **will live wherever the river flows**. There will be large numbers of fish**, because this water flows there and makes the salt water fresh; so where the river flows,everything will live**.(Ezekiel 47:9) New International Version.*

The anointing brings life to dead situations. Allow the river or rivers of living water to bring life wherever you go. Let the river or rivers of living water that is in you bring refreshing and vitality. Wherever you go make a positive difference.

Please take note that when I speak of flowing in the anointing I am speaking of releasing the anointing that is in you and upon you.

When Barnabas came to Antioch, he flowed in the anointing that was upon him. *For he was a good man, and **full of the Holy Ghost** (this of course is speaking of the anointing) and of faith: and **much people was added unto the Lord**. (Acts 11:24.)*KJV The result of Barnabas flowing in the anointing that was upon him was that many people were added to the Lord. *What results are being manifested through the anointing that is upon you? Do you really have the anointing or are you claiming to have the anointing?*

3. Be Consistent

Take heed unto thyself, and unto the doctrine;**continue in them**: for in doing this *thou shalt **both save thy self and them that hear thee**. (1Timothy4:16)*KJV Be consistent in doing what is good.

***Never lag in zeal** and **in earnest endeavor; be aglow** and **burning with the Spirit**,serving the Lord.(Romans 12:11)Amplied Bible Classic Edition(AMPC)*

Never lag in zeal. Never means never because that is what never means! Be aglow and burning with the Spirit. The anointing fills you with the zeal of the Lord. That zeal must burn fervently!

The release of the anointing must continue unhindered. Consistence in releasing the anointing is of utmost importance if you are to be a blessing to your generation.

Be watchful in all things. Stay pure doctrinally. Avoid getting on the bandwagon of every questionable wind of doctrine that comes on the scene.

Avoid getting into situations where no one can put breaks on you should you get on a wrong path.Operate under good accountability structures.

4. Staying In The Field Of Your Assignment!

In Zimbabwe, There is a place called Honde Valley where bananas grow very well. While bananas can grow in all kinds of places,they grow best in Honde Valley!

Your field of assignment is where you manifest the fruit of your anointing best!

One of the most powerful secrets to effectively releasing the anointing that is upon you is to operate in the field that the Lord has assigned you to operate in.

Bishop Tudor Bismark and his wife Pastor Chichi Bismark are the founders and Senior Pastors of New Life Covenant Church in Harare, Zimbabwe. This local church is the headquarters of Jabula New Life Ministries International whose network is global.

Bishop Tudor Bismark has been anointed by the Lord to serve as an Apostolic Father and mentor and Overseer to over 900 ministers around the world. Bishop Tudor Bismark also serves as the Chairman of the Council of African Apostles.

His field of operation is multidimensional in nature because he serves in all the roles that I have mentioned. His ministry is not limited to just one locality. Not everyone serves in this way and each one of us must learn to flow in the grace given us.

Some people are graced with a certain message to the Body of Christ. Some people maybe specially anointed to reach the lost for Christ (*evangelists*). And some people are multi graced and very versatile.

Due to the anointing that is upon Bishop Tudor Bismark, he does not struggle to travel around the world. Invitations to minister abound because he is a much sought after minister in the Body of Christ.

Where you are anointed, you operate gracefully and that with tangible results. However, where you are not anointed, disgrace may follow. And it can be a struggle to get even meagre results.

Paul was aware of his assigned field of operation which was to minister primarily to the Gentiles.

That's why he said, *"God gave His grace to me, the least of all God's people, to preach the good news about the immeasurable riches of Christ* **to the Gentiles***"(Ephesians 3:8) Common English Bible*

I am saying all this especially for you Gentiles. **God has appointed me as the apostle to the Gentiles.** *I stress this.(Ephesians 3:8)New Living Translation.*

Galatians 2:7, 8 (KJV)

7. But contrariwise, **when they saw that the gospel of the uncircumcision was committed unto me**, *as* **the gospel of the circumcision was unto Peter**;

8. (For He that **wrought effectually in Peter to the apostleship of circumcision**, *the same was mighty in me toward the Gentiles)*

Paul was very successful among the Gentiles because that was the field that the Lord had assigned him to labor in. In other words, he was anointed to preach primarily to the Gentiles. Here and there he did preach to the Jews but he did not experience the same kind of success as when laboring among the Gentiles.

On the other hand Peter was assigned to minister to the Jews and was very successful among the Jews because that was the field that the Lord had assigned him to labor in. Peter was anointed to preach to the Jews. Here and there he did minister to the Gentiles but the results among the Gentiles were meagre compared to the results among the Jews.

The anointing flows best in the field of your assignment.

But when he(king Uzziah)was strong, **his heart was lifted up to his destruction***: for he transgressed against the LORD his God, and went into the temple of the Lord to burn incense upon the altar of incense.(2 Chronicles 26:16)KJV*

When king Uzziah decided to offer incense in the temple of God, the priests withstood him and clearly told him," *"It appertaineth* **not unto thee**, *Uzziah, to burn incense unto the Lord,* **but to the priests the sons of Aaron**, **that are consecrated to burn incense***: go out of the sanctuary; for thou hast trespassed; neither] shall it be for thine honor from the Lord God" (2 Chronicles 26:18)KJV*

2 Chronicles 26:19-21(KJV)

19. Then Uzziah was wroth, and had **a censer in his hand** *to burn incense: and while he was wroth with the priests, the leprosy even rose up in his forehead before the priests in the house of the LORD, from beside the incense altar.*

20. And Azariah the chief priest, and all the priests, looked upon him, and behold, he was leprous in his forehead, and they thrust him out from thence; yea, himself hasted also to go out, because the LORD had smitten him.

21. And Uzziah the king was a leper unto the day of his death, and dwelt in a several house, being a leper; for he was cut off from the house of the LORD: and Jotham his son was over the king's house, judging the people of the land.

King Uzziah as a king had the anointing and authority to rule over the entire nation. *In other words he had a **sceptre of rulership in his hand** but from nowhere he just decided to exchange that for a **censer for burning incense in the temple!***

However, that did not automatically give him authority to offer incense on the altar of sacrifice in the temple since he did not have the priestly anointing to function in that role.

Know the jurisdiction of your anointing and work there until God moves you to another field of His choice. Do not presume to overstep the limits of your anointing without God's approval and leading.

2 Corinthians 10:13-15 Amplified Bible Classic Edition(AMPC)

*13. We, on the other hand, will **not boast beyond our legitimate province** and **proper limits**, but [of our commission which] God Has **allotted us** as our **measuring line** and which **reaches** and **includes even you.***

***14.** For we are **not overstepping the limits** of our province **and stretching beyond our ability to reach,** as though we reached not **(had no legitimate mission)** to you, for we were[the very first] to come even as far to you with the goodnews of Christ.*

15.** We do not boast therefore, **beyond our proper limit,** even other men's labors, but we have the hope and confident expectation that as your faith continues to grow our field among you maybe **greatly enlarged, still within our limits of our commission.

Do not overstep your measure of rule. Let *true humility* help you to function within your measure of rule.

Every anointing has its particular measure of operation. Overstepping that measure without God's sanction can get one in trouble.

Don't allow the sin of pride to make you go beyond your scope of operation because *Those who walk in pride He (God) is able to abase and humble. Daniel 4:37*(b) *Amplified Bible Classic Edition (AMPC)*

We must be so sensitive to the Lord that when He wants us to extend or go beyong our usual scope of operation, we move accordingly and not get stuck in the rut! Operating in the anointing demands that kind of sensitivity!

When God's promotion comes,one must be found co operative and obedient!

5. Operate In The Proportion Of Your Faith!

Romans 12:6-8 (KJV)

6. Having then gifts differing according to the grace (or anointing) that is given to us, whether prophecy, **let us prophesy according to the proportion of faith;**

7. Or **ministry,** *let us wait on our ministering: or* **he that teacheth***, on teaching;***Or he that exhorteth***, on exhortation:* **he that giveth***, let him do it with simplicity;* **he that ruleth***, with diligence;* **he that sheweth mercy***, with cheerfulness.*

If it is prophecy prophesy according to the proportion of your faith. ***In other words don't bite more than you can chew! Don't go beyond the proportion of your faith. Don't be under pressure to impress and overdo things lest you end up operating in the flesh!***

The Lord may desire to increase the proportion of your faith in the area of your anointing. And if it is the Lord that is increasing your faith capacity, then stretch out and do it!

Sometimes your usual measure of faith can become a hindrance when it is the Lord's time for you to go beyond your usual measure of faith.

6. Grieve Not The Holy Spirit

And grieve not the Holy Spirit of God, whereby ye are sealed unto the day of redemption. (Ephesians 4:30)KJV

To grieve the Holy Spirit is to wound Him and to sadden Him. When we walk in impurity and disobedience we certainly grieve the Holy Spirit.

Some of the things that grieve the Holy Spirit are things found in the preceding verse which says;*Let no corrupt communication proceed out of your mouth, but that which is good to the use of edifying, that it may minister grace unto the hearers.(Ephesians 4:29)* Avoid corrupt communication or words that tear or criticise other people. They grieve the Holy Spirit who is the Spirit of grace. *(Hebrews 10:29)KJV*

Again some of the things that grieve the Holy Spirit are found in the verses after our text. Here are the verses:

*Let **all bitterness**, and **wrath,** and **anger**, and **clamour**, and **evil speaking**, be put away from you, with all malice: And **be ye kind one to another, tender-hearted, forgiving one another**, even as God for Christ's sake hath forgiven you.(Ephesians 4:31,32)KJV*

When the Holy Spirit is grieved He does not operate effectively in our lives as this tends to quench Him in His operations.

The Holy Spirit is very sensitive to how we treat Him and other people. We must learn to avoid doing things that grieve Him so that we can effectively flow in the anointing lest we quench the Holy Spirit and consequently loose the anointing. The Bible admonishes us: *Quench not the Spirit. (1Thessalonians 5:19)KJV*

7. Live A life Of Obedience To The Holy Spirit

*[If we live by the [Holy]Spirit, let us also walk by the Spirit. [If by the Spirit we have our life in God, **let us go forward walking in line, our conduct controlled by the Spirit]**. Galatians 5:23 Amplified Bible Classic (AMPC)*

*But I say, **walk and live [habitually] in the [Holy] Spirit [responsive to and controlled and guided by the Spirit]**. Galatians 5:16(a) Amplified Bible Classic Edition (AMPC)*

What these verses are stressing is the need to live a life of obedience to the Holy Spirit and yielding to His control.

Samson Lost the Anointing

Samson was powerfully anointed by the Holy Spirit. However, he continually walked in disobedience to the Lord and yet the Holy Spirit continued to come upon him and Samson continued doing amazing miracles by the power of the Holy Spirit.

Every time he shook himself the Holy Spirit would come upon him mightily. It got to a place where he took some things for granted. Then one day he shook himself but *he wist not that the Lord was departed from him. (Judges 16:20)KJV*

That got him into deep trouble as *the Philistines took him, and put out his eyes, and brought him down to Gaza, and bound him with fetters of brass; and he did grind in the prison house.(Judges 16:21) KJV*

The Philistines turned him into their grinding and sporting machine! Samson was anointed to be a deliverer but now he was grinding for the Philistines instead of delivering the Children of Israel from the bondage and oppression of the Philistines.

Samson Recovered The Anointing

Perhaps you have lost the anointing. God is a God of restoration. *Remember therefore from whence thou art fallen, and repent, and do the first works…"* (Revelation 2:5)KJV Identify where you fell and repent.

Thank God that Samson got another chance.

Some people never recover from their fall. King Saul did not recover and died tragically and David made this lamentation over king Saul:

*Ye mountains of Gilboa, let there be no dew, neither let there be rain, upon you, nor fields of offerings: for there the shield of the mighty is vilely cast away, the shield of Saul, **as though he had not been anointed with oil**.(2samuel 1:21)KJV*

Judges 16:28, 30(KJV)

28. And *Samson called unto the LORD, and said, O Lord GOD, remember me, I pray thee, and strengthen me, I pray thee, only this once, O God, that I maybe at once avenged of the Philistines for my two eyes.*

30. *And Samson said, Let me die with the Philistines. And he bowed himself with all his might; and the house fell upon the lords, and upon all the people that were therein. So the dead which he slew at his death were more than they which he slew in his life.*

Even though Samson eventually died, he however fulfilled his God given purpose because he killed more people in his death than in his life time through the power of the anointing of God.

8. Be Continuously Filled With The Holy Spirit

And be not drunk with wine, wherein is excess; but be filled with the Spirit. (Ephesians 5:18)KJV

Getting drunk with wine can cause one to loose sound judgement. This is one reason why driving under the influence of alchohol is prohibited as this can result unsound judgement with serious consquences.

Howefer,being filled with the Holy Spirit will cause one to walk in the ways of God because the Holy Spirit guides us in the ways of God.

On the surface it seems like Ephesians 5:18 is speaking of a singular infilling of the Holy Spirit. However the real thought behind this verse in the original Greek language is to be be filled time and again or rather being continuously filled with the Holy Spirit.

It is not a once for all infilling but experiencing infillings of the Holy Spirit again and again and again! You should never get to where you think you have arrived and do not need to be filled again!

And they were **all filled** with the Holy Ghost, and began to speak with other tongues, as the Spirit gave them utterance.*(Acts 2:4)KJV*

The early disciples faced persecution after the lame man at the Beautiful Gate was healed. They gathered for prayer and the Word of God tells us that *They were all **filled with the Holy Ghost**, and they spake the Word of God with boldness (Acts 4:31)KJV* Among this group of people were people who were filled with the Holy Ghost on the day of Pentecost.

*Then Peter, **filled with the Holy Ghost**, said unto them, Ye rulers of the people, and elders of Israel…(Acts 4:8)KJV* Take note that Peter was among the people who had been filled with the Holy Ghost on the day of Pentecost besides being among the people who were filled in Acts 4:31. Peter experienced several infillings of the Holy Spirit and so must we if we do not want to end up losing the anointing that is upon our lives.

CONCLUSION

Take yourself as a conduit. Ensure that there are no clogs that can hinder the flow of the living waters of the anointing from flowing through you.

Make sure the inlet is allowing the inflow and the outlet of the conduit is also allowing the outflow of the living waters of the anointing to flow out without hindrance.

John 7:38, 39(KJV)

38. He that believeth on me, as the scriptures hath said, out of his belly (innermost being) **shall flow rivers of living water.**

*39. (But this spake he of **the Spirit**, which they that believe on Him should receive: for the Holy Ghost was not yet given; because that Jesus was not yet glorified.* The Holy Ghost anointing is here portrayed as rivers of living water. Allow those rivers to flow as you release the anointing that is upon you for the benefit of other people.

Where you are anointed, you operate gracefully and that with tangible results. However, where you are not anointed, disgrace may follow and it is a struggle to get even meagre results

Chapter Eight

BEWARE OF MERCHANDISING THE ANOINTING!

What is merchandising the anointing?

According to the Macmillan Dictionary, *"Merchandise are goods that people buy and sell"*.

Merchandising the anointing is acquiring profit, fame, or advantage by illegitimately and unethically exploiting the anointing or even what is purported to be the anointing.

It is important to know that no one is immune from the possibility of merchandising the anointing. Merchandising the anointing comes in various forms some of which are extremely subtle to discern.

It's a phenomenon that we must avoid by all means because the consequences of engaging in this practice are quiet devastating.

1. Don't Merchandise The Anointing!

In 2Kings Chapter five we find the story of Naaman who was the captain of the host of the king of Syria. Naaman was a leper who happened to go to Prophet Elisha to seek divine healing at the advice of his wife's maid.

After experiencing his miraculous healing, Naaman came with a blessing to give to the man of God that consisted of *ten talents of silver, and six thousand pieces of gold, and ten changes of raiment. (2Kings 5:5)KJV*

2Kings 5:15-16, 20-27(KJV)

*15.And he returned to the man of God, he and all his company, and came, and stood before him: and he said, Behold, now I know that there is no God in all the earth, but in Israel: now therefore, I pray thee, **take a blessing of thy servant.***

*16. **But he said, As the LORD liveth, before whom I stand, I will receive none. And he urged him to take it: but he refused.***

*20.But Gehazi, the servant of Elisha the man of God, said, Behold, my master hath spared Naaman the Syrian, in not receiving at his hands that which he brought: but, as the LORD liveth, **I will run after him, and take somewhat of him**.(2Kings 5:20)*

21.So Gehazi followed after Naaman. And when Naaman saw him running after him, he lighted down from the chariot to meet him, and said, is all well?

22. And he said, all is well. My master hath sent me, saying, Behold, even now there be come to me from mount Ephraim two young men of the sons of the prophets: give them I pray thee, a talent of silver, and two changes of garments.

23.And Naaman said, Be content, take two talents. And he urged him, and bound two talents of silver in two bags, with two changes of garments, and laid them upon two of his servants; and they bare them before him.

24. And when he came to the tower, he took them from their hand, and bestowed them in the house: and he let them go, and they departed.

25. But he went in, and stood before his master.

And Elisha said unto him, whence comest thou, Gehazi? And he said, Thy servant went no whither (nowhere).

26. And he said unto him, Went not mine heart with thee, when the man turned again from his chariot to meet thee? Is this a time to receive money, and to receive garments, and olive yards, and vineyards, and sheep, and oxen, and menservants, and maidservants?

*27. **The leprosy therefore of Naaman shall cleave unto thee and unto thy seed for ever. And he went out from his presence a leper as white as snow.***

In 2 Kings 5:26(KJV)Elisha said to Gehazi, "***Is this a time** to receive **money,** and to receive **garments,** and **olive yards**, and **sheep**, and **oxen**, and **menservants**, and **maidservants?**"* thus shedding light on what was in Gehazi's mind.

I am very sure that Gehazi heard what his master had said when he declined to take the blessing of the gifts from Naaman. Elisha had said, *"As the LORD liveth, before whom I stand, I will receive none. And he (Naaman) urged him to take it: but he refused"* (2 Kings 5:16)KJV

Why would Gehazi blatantly go against the philosophy displayed by his master? *But Gehazi, the servant of Elisha the man of God, said, Behold, my master hath spared Naaman the Syrian, in not receiving at his hands that which he brought: but, as the LORD liveth, I will run after him, and **take somewhat of him**.(2Kings 5:20)KJV*

Gehazi merchandised the anointing by illegitimately and unethically benefiting from what the anointing had accomplished.

This was also gross insubordination and disrespect for his master. As a servant Gehazi was supposed to simply follow what his master had said!

Or if he had some questions concerning his master's refusal to take the gifts, he should have simply asked his master about this episode. I am very sure that Elisha would have enlightened Gehazi as to why he had refused to take those gifts.

Operating in the anointing demands that we be sensitive to the Holy Spirit's leading and promptings. It takes a lot of sensitivity to know which gift to receive and which gift to decline!

Paul was not after gifts that some churches gave him but his main concern was fruit that would abound to their account. He was more interested in being a blessing to them than getting a blessing from them!

Philippians 4:16, 17(KJV)

16. For even in Thessalonica ye sent once and again unto my necessity.

*17. **Not because I desire a gift: but I desire fruit that may abound to your account.*** That's the attitude we must emulate in our lives and ministries.

In 2015 I went to the American Embassy to obtain a visa to for a gospel mission to the USA. The lady who was interviewing me said, "So you are a minister of the gospel? You are in one of the most lucrative professions in this country!"

My heart sank at these words. "Is this how far being a minister of the gospel is being perceived by some people?" I thought within myself as I kindly told her that it was not so with me and many other ministers of the gospel.

We must not get involved in questionable and unethical ways of acquiring money, gifts and possessions. God's Word admonishes us that *Godliness with contentment is great gain. (1Timothy 6:6)KJV*

2. Do Not Allow People To Make Merchandise of You!

In 2 Peter 2:3(KJV) Peter warns of teachers who *through covetousness shall with feigned words **make merchandise of you.*** In the New International Version this verse is rendered as follows:*in their greed these teachers will **exploit you with fabricated stories.***

There are some ministers whose main aim is to get money out of your pockets into theirs by making merchandise of you. This is usually done by fabricated stories that are spiced with scriptures that are often twisted out of their proper context and meaning.

The gullible swallow these lies both line and sinker like a baited fish that does not realize it is in for a catch!

*Which have **forsaken the right way**, and **are gone astray**, following the way of Balaam the son of Bosor, **who loved the wages of unrighteousness** (2Peter2:15) KJV Balaam was a prophet for profit.* Do not walk in the ways of Balaam.

The Apostle Paul says, *"Unlike so many, **we do not peddle the Word of God for profit.** On the contrary, **in Christ we speak before God with sincerity, as those sent from God**" 2 Corinthians 2:17 (New International Version) **Men and women sent from God are not*** *interested in peddling the Word of God for profit or for gifts only, but they desire fruit that abound to the account of those that they minister to.*

We thank the Lord that there are many ministers who actually sacrifice a lot for the people that they have spiritual oversight over. Indeed there are many ministers who do not earn decent salaries but in spite of that still wholeheartedly serve the Lord and those under their care.

It is a fact that there are many ministers who do not merchandise the anointing but serve with a ready mind and a willing heart. It is regrettable that at times every minister ends up being painted with the same brush with those ministers who have done things wrongly.

This is not written to condemn anyone but to encourage us to do the right thing as this glorifies the Lord.A higher standard is expected of those that represent the Lord. This is just that *Ye walk worthy of the vocation wherewith ye are called.(Ephesians 4:1)KJV*

Merchandising the anointing can easily lead someone into sins of covetousness and idolatry without realising it. These are deadly sins that cause shipwrecks and drawn some servants of the Lord into perdition.

Covetousness is a deep desire to possess what does not belong to you. *Thou shalt not covet thy neighbour's house; thou shalt not covet thy neighbour's wife, or his manservant, or his maidservant, or his ox, or his ass(or donkey), or anything that is thy neighbour's. (Exodus 20:16)King James Version*

Covetousness is an awful sin because it is equated with idolatry. *Mortify therefore your members which are upon the earth; fornication, uncleanliness, inordinate affection, evil concupiscence, and covetousness, which is idolatry.(Colossians 3:5)KJV*

God's Word forbids us to covet other people's possessions and yet how many people are coveting other people's possessions, positions or properties?

Steer clear of the love of money and any unethical ways of making money.

1Timothy 6:9-10(KJV)

9. **But they that will be rich fall into temptation** *and* **a snare,** *and into* **many foolish** *and* **hurtful lusts,** *which* **drawn men in destruction and perdition.**

10. **for the love of money is the root of all evil***: which while some have* **coveted after***, they have* **erred from the faith***, and* **pierced themselves through with many sorrows***.*

At the core of merchandising the anointing is the love of money, coventeoudness, craftiness and a lack of the fear of the Lord.

3. Beware Of The Sin Of Familiarity!

I think Gehazi must have gotten too familiar with his master, Prophet Elisha. He knew that Prophet Elisha did not operate in the word of knowledge at all times. And because of that familiarity he took the gamble to fabricate that story supposing that his master was not likely to function in the word of knowledge that day.

The gamble backfired because Elisha functioned in the word of knowledge with a precision that probably took Gehazi by surprise.

Pastor Tom Deuschle, the Senior Pastor of Celebration Church in Borrowdale, Harare, Zimbabwe, in his book entitled *"First Fruits"* says, *"One of the greatest sins committed against appointed leaders in the church today is that of familiarity"*

Familiarity breeds contempt. Don't become too familiar with the man or woman of God in your life.

We must have a healthy respect for the man and woman of God in our lives. And by all means do not go to the extreme of worshipping the man or woman of God as this is dangerous both for you and the man or woman of God in your life.

He that receiveth a prophet in the name of a prophet shall receive a prophet's reward. (Matthew 10:41)KJV It is ironic that Naaman believed and respected Prophet Elisha while his protégé and servant did not. Naaman received the benefit of the anointing that was upon Prophet Elisha. Unfortunately, all Gehazi received was a curse of the very leprosy that Naaman was healed of!

Merchandising the anointing might look like a lucrative business but it is a very dangerous activity to get involved in.

4. Let Integrity Guide You In Your Actions

*I will behave **wisely** and follow the **way** of **integrity**. When will you come to me? I will walk in my house in integrity and with a **blameless heart**. (Psalm 101:2) Amplified Bible(AMP)*
According to the Merriam-Webster English Dictionary **integrity**

1. Is the firm adherence to a code especially moral or artistic values
   Incorruptibility
2. *Is an unimpaired condition.*
   Soundness

3. *Is the quality of being complete or undivided.*
    Completeness

Integrity is of greater value than most people care to realise. Integrity is the state of being incorrupt,sound and complete and untainted with unethical practices.

A person of integrity is a person whose character is the same in secret and in public. Such a person is absolutely honest and can be relied upon. Such a person hates corruption which has destroyed the fabric of our societies.

Let integrity guide your actions. It is one of the most powerful values that can guard you from being sucked up in merchandising the anointing.

*The **integrity of the upright guideth them**; but **the crookedness of the unfaithful destroyeth them**. Proverbs 11:3 Darby Bible Translation (DBT)*

Corruption has destroyed many organisations in our time. Integrity is a rare virtue that we must not allow to go into extinction because it's a virtue we ascribe to as the people of God.

A person of integrity is opposed to corruption and wants to do things uprightly. The unfaithful and crooked do things in a corrupt way and end up destroyed by their corrupt ways. The crookedness of the unfaithful and corrupt is a trap that ends up destroying the unfaithful and corrupt.

Integrity Will Preserve You

Let integrity and uprightness preserve me; for I wait on thee. (Psalm25:21)KJV

Real Security Is Premised On Integrity

*Whoever walks in **integrity walks securely**, but whoever takes **crooked paths will be found out**. Proverbs 10:9(New International Version)*

*The New Living Translation puts this verse in this manner: People with integrity **walk safely**, but those who follow **crooked paths will slip and fall.***

What Gehazi did not realise was that he was trading in the spirit through his corrupt actions. The merchandise he got in the end was leprosy for himself and unfortunately also for his innocent descendants!

The leprosy of Naaman shall cleave unto thee, and unto thy seed for ever. And he went from his presence a leper as white as snow. (2 Kings 5:27)KJV

We must renounce walking in the ways of Gehazi.

*But we have renounced the things hidden because of shame, **not walking in craftiness or adulterating the Word of God**, but by the manifestation of **truth** commending ourselves to every man's conscience in the sight of God.2 Corinthians 4:2 New American Standard Bible (NASB)*

May we receive the grace to serve God acceptably with reverence and godly fear.

*Wherefore we receiving a kingdom which cannot be moved,let us have grace, whereby we may serve God **acceptably** with **reverence** and **godly fear**. For our God is a consuming fire. (Hebrews 12:28,29)KJV*

5. The Gift Of God Can Not Be Purchased By Money!

In Acts chapter 8 Simon tried to merchandise the anointing. After observing that through the laying on of hands by Peter and John people received the Holy Ghost (or the anointing) he offered them money so that he could be able to do the same thing that he witnessed Peter and John doing.

*Simon said "**Give me also this power** that on whomever I lay hands; he may receive the Holy Ghost." (Acts 8:19)KJV*

*But Peter said unto him, **Thy money perish with thee, because thou hast thought that the gift of God maybe purchased with money"** (Acts 8:19).KJV*

What Simon did was so deplorable that a new word called "**simony**" was coined from this encounter. The meaning of this dirty word is underpinned by merchandising the anointing or illegitimately acquiring profit, position, fame, power by trading something in matters pertaining to sacred things.

Simon's background is described in the verses that follow:

Acts 8:9, 10 (KJV)

*9. There was a certain man, called Simon, which beforetime in the same city **used sorcery**, and **bewitched the people of Samaria giving out that himself was some great one.***

*10. To whom they all gave heed, from the least to the greatest, saying, **This man is the great power of God.***

Simon was a sorcerer which is another word for a witch, a wizard or a magician. Such people use the power of evil spirits to do their work. In simple words he operated in demonic anointing.

Simon had acquired fame that he was the great power of God in the city of Samaria. That is merchandising the anointing big time!

Some ministers of God in their desperation for the power of God have ended up going to unethical sources to acquire power. God forbid!

But when Philip came on the scene, *Then Simon himself believed also: and when he was baptized, he continued with Philip, and **wondered, beholding the miracles and signs which were done**. (Acts 8:13)KJV*

In other words, Simon was actually mesmerised by the miracles and signs that were being performed through Philip's ministry!

Remember that Simon was now a believer who believed the gospel that Philip preached. However, the tendency to merchandise the anointing seemed to be a normal practice with him!

Instead of wanting to do things the right way now that he was a Christian, Simon offered money to the apostles so that whomever he laid his hands on would receive the Holy Spirit!

Peter's rebuke of Simon was actually a curse!*"Thy money perish with thee, because thou hast thought that the gift of God maybe purchased with money" (Acts 8:20)KJV.* This was pretty hot stuff! So hot that Simon said to Peter, *"Pray ye to the Lord for me, that none of these things which ye have spoken come upon me" (Acts 8:24)KJV*

Merchandising the anointing is a deadlyl activity. Therefore avoid it by all means!

6. Do Not Be Under Undue Pressure To Perform!

Ananias and Sapphira made an impression that they were great givers until Peter confronted each of them thus exposing their dishonesty behavior.

But Peter said, Ananias, why hath Satan filled thine heart to lie to the Holy Ghost, and to keep part of the price of the land?(Acts 5:3)KJV

Peter told her (Sapphira)*How is it that ye have agreed together to tempt the Spirit of the Lord? (Acts5:9)KJV*

Don't be under pressure to perform or keep up with others that may seem to be doing well lest this leads you into merchandising the anointing!

Of course it is good to be genuinely challenged to excel in your endeavors. Just don't overplay this to your detriment! At times the temptation to do just that can be very great.

Unfortunately they were not on the same level of grace with Barnabas. They ended up faking it. This behavior ended up costing their very lives!

7. The Anointing Gives Us The Power To Thrive Under Any Situation!

Paul was so seasoned that he was able to survive both in abundance and in need without any problem.

I have experienced times of need and times of abundance. In any and every circumstance I have learned the secret of contentment, either I go satisfied or hungry have plenty or nothing. Philippians 4:12(NET Bible)

Philippians 4:13(KJV) *"I can do all things through Christ which strengtheneth me"* has been grossly quoted out of context by many well-meaning Christians.

The context of what Paul was saying in this verse was that he could handle any circumstance that he found himself in (times of need or times of abundance) through the power of Christ which is the anointing.

The anointing is there to give us the power to thrive in times of abundance or in times of need, in good times or in bad times!

CONCLUSION

*But seek ye first the kingdom of God,and His righteousness; and **all these things shall be added unto you.** (Matthew 6:33) KJV*

We can get into all kinds of wrong things when we take it upon ourselves to do the adding instead of allowing God to do it in His own way and in His own time!

1Peter 5:1-3 Amplified Bible Classic Edition(AMPC)

1.*I **warn** and **counsel** the **elders among** you(**the pastors and spiritual guides of the church**) as a fellow elder and as an eyewitness[called to testify] of the sufferings of Christ, as well as a sharer in the glory (the honour and splendour) that is to be revealed(disclosed, unfolded):*

*2. Tend (**nurture, guard, guide and fold**) the flock of God that is [your responsibility], **not by coercion** or **constraint, but willingly: not dishonorably motivated by the advantages** and **profits** [belonging to the office], but **eagerly** and **cheerfully**;*

*3. **Not domineering** [as arrogant, dictatorial, and overbearing persons] **over those in your charge, but being examples (patterns and models of Christian living) to the flock** (the congregation).*

In each one of us is a leader. Let the leader in you willingly serve the Lord, not for what you can get but for what you can give!

Always aim to do the right thing for the right reason

References

Biblesoft. Biblesoft's New Exhaustive Strong's Numbers and Concordance with Expanded Greek-Hebrew Dictionary. . Biblesoft, 2006.

—. Matthew Henry's Commentary on the Whole Bible. PC Study Bible Formatted Electronic Database, 2006.

Excellent, Paul. "When purpose is not known." BecomExcellence. <becomexcellence. blogspot.com>.

Maldonado, Guillermo. How to walk in the Supernatural power of God. Miami: Whitaker House, 2013.

Merriam-webster Dictionary. Merriam-webster Dictionary. <www.merriam-webster.com/ dictionary/annoint>.

Nahum, Rosario. The secrets of the anointing. Chicago: Maranatha Publications, 1994.

Pinterest. "Explore Best Quotes, Famous Quotes and more." Pinterest. <pinterest.com>.

Rich, Tracey R. <u>Judaism 101.</u> 1995.

Thayer, Joseph H. <u>Thayer's Greek English Lexicon of the New Testament.</u> Hendrickson Publishers, 1995.

Webster's Revised Unabridged Dictionary. "Webster's Revised Unabridged Dictionary." 1998.

Berry Dambaza's first book is full of revelations of how God
can use you to effectively impact others for Christ.

How To Become A Vessel That God Can Use

Kirimi Barine says *"There is no better joy than to know that you have discovered your
purpose and that you are a vessel that God is using every day of your life. Strive to know
how by reading this book"*

This book can be purchased on the publisher's website www.evangelpublishing.org or you
can contact the author at berry.dambaz@gmail.com

Help Spread The Word About This Book: How To Receive And Release The Anointing.

Please tell others in the circle of your influence and

- Please leave me a helpful review on Amazon and other Digital Platforms where you
  may have purchased a copy of this book.
- Purchase additional copies to give away as gifts to your friends, relatives or
  workmates etc.
- Write about How to receive and release the anointing on your blog. Post brief excerpts
  to your social media sites such as:Facebook,Twitter,Pinterest,Instgraham, etc.
- You can order copies of this book at …

About The Author

Berry Dambaza is a dynamic power packed preacher of the gospel with a life changing and life impacting ministry. He has been divinely endowed with a unique and powerful gift of ministering the Word of God that captivates listeners' attention. Through his God given ministry, many people have experienced salvation, miracles, healing and deliverance. Others have been baptized in the Holy Spirit with the evidence of speaking in other tongues while others have experienced dramatic encounters with God's supernatural power.

In 1984, Berry graduated from the Pentecostal Bible College (now known as Pan African Christian College) which is based in Harare, Zimbabwe, with a Ministerial Diploma. He went on with his educational pursuit and later graduated with a B. A. Degree in Bible Theology in 2005 from the same college. Berry Dambaza is also a writer, motivational speaker, conference speaker, mentor, life coach and an entrepreneur. He has a blog called The Arena For Divine Solutions through which he ministers the Word of God to an ever increasing worldwide audience.

He is the Senior Minister (Pastor) of Upper Room Ministries, a vibrant church in the city Centre of Harare, the capital city of Zimbabwe. Upper Room Ministries is a church of the Pentecostal Assemblies of Zimbabwe (PAOZ), a nationwide church with many local churches in Zimbabwe.

After graduating from Bible College, he worked in a number of places where he served several organizations in different capacities. Among these organizations are Rivers of Life Ministries in Harare as an Associate Pastor, Miracle Rain Crusades in Harare as an Associate Evangelist, Calvary Bible Church in Marondera as an Assistant Pastor, PAOZ Marondera Assembly as an Assistant Pastor and as the Pastor of PAOZ Kambuzuma Pentecostal Church in Harare. He then came to Upper Room Ministries initially as an Assistant Pastor in 1996.He was later installed as the Senior Pastor of PAOZ -Upper Room Ministries in the year 2000. He is a former board member of the Village of Hope and he sits on the Advisory Board of Hope for All Nations Ministries International and is a board member of Miracle Helping Hand Foundation. He is a former Provincial Overseer of PAOZ Harare Province as well as the former PAOZ National Men's Director. Berry Dambaza is a member of the PAOZ Bishops' Council. He is the Bishop responsible for Finance, Administration, Evangelism and Church Planting in the PAOZ.

He is married to Sithembeni Dambaza who is also an Assistant Pastor (Minister) at PAOZ Upper Room Ministries and she is also a former PAOZ National Women's Director and a member of the PAOZ Apostolic Council. They have two daughters (Oreen and Oretha) and two sons (Osborn and Oracle).

Berry Dambaza has extensively ministered the Word of God in Zimbabwe and has been privileged by the grace of God to minister the Word of God in Zambia, South Africa, Kenya, Malawi, Botswana, The DRC, India, Israel and the USA.

Let Us Keep In Touch

You can reach me by writing me at <u>berry.dambaz@gmail.com</u>

You can access other inspiring messages and teachings and life building products by entering ***The Arena Of Divine Solutions*** which is my blog by logging on my website located at <u>www.docberrydambaza.com</u>

Printed in the United States
By Bookmasters